How to Furnish

OLD AMERICAN HOUSES

Unusually fine example of an 18th Century living room, showing its handsome fireplace wall with pilasters and raised panels.

How to Furnish

OLD AMERICAN
HOUSES

by

Henry Lionel Williams and
Ottalie K. Williams

BONANZA BOOKS • NEW YORK

FOR

Leslie Gordon Phillips

This edition published by Bonanza Books,
a division of Crown Publishers, Inc.,
by arrangement with Farrar, Straus & Giroux, Inc.
d   e   f

CONTENTS

FOREWORD: *Old Houses for New Ones*

BOOK ONE: *Yesterday*

FOREWORD

Old Houses for New Ones

Just about a hundred years ago, steam power launched America's industrial age and brought with it new wealth, luxury, and tasteless extravagance in domestic architecture and furnishing. Soon after the dawn of the twentieth century the era of tasseled upholstery, plush draperies, and hand-painted lamp globes gave way to the all-American Mission style furniture so well adapted to the scrollwork and colored glass that were the latest architectural fads for middle-class houses. From the somber, pretentious Victorian, the architecture gradually assumed a more cosmopolitan air as Swiss chalets, Spanish casitas, and Mediterranean villas sprang up alongside English cottages in new subdivisions all over the United States.

From these and many another experiment in designing houses for Americans, the more forward-looking architects and builders hoped to develop a new style of small house that was peculiarly American, but to date they have not notably succeeded. Some of the more recent types of modern houses come nearer to expressing the American spirit but even they do not wholly achieve the ideal of convenience combined with charm, of utility with eye-appeal, or provide the restful, homey atmosphere that is hard to describe but easy to recognize when encountered.

Today more and more Americans of moderate means are turning to copies and adaptations of Old American houses—houses built during the late 17th and entire 18th centuries. In spite of all the "advances" made in American architecture since A.D. 1800, it is these types of houses that most Americans prefer, and which they can build in the confident assurance that the style will not become obsolete for many years to come.

The history of house furnishing in America has closely paralleled that of its domestic architecture. From the fateful 1840s, beauty declined even when comfort did not. Indeed, in the whole of the arts except painting, degeneration accompanied the rise of industry. Not only the skill to create and perpetuate beautiful utilitarian things appears to have been lost, but also the desire. New methods brought new manufacturing possibilities and art became the much abused servant of industry in devising products that could be turned out en masse. The craftsman, concerned with the quality of the things he made, was replaced by the artisan interested only in how many he could produce. And so, even to the present day, little that is available for the furnishing of small houses excels the handicraft of America's early craftsman, and, later, the copies of the less ornate products of Chippendale, Hepplewhite, Sheraton, and Phyfe.

What the modern age has contributed are the materials and techniques of building old-style houses durably and soundly and providing for them well-made furniture that has all the charm and feeling of the old-time pieces. These things being so, the most satisfying American small homes today are the Old American houses, whether of the Early American, Georgian, or Greek Revival styles, furnished with the traditional designs of furniture with which they have been associated since the earliest times.

This is the basic premise on which all that follows in this book is founded. But there are a number of other points to be considered in furnishing the Old American house. Houses that are homes should grow and develop with the passing years. They should, in many respects, be adapted to changing ideas in living, and provide comforts and conveniences that were not available when they were originally built or first designed.

These things can be done without spoiling the "feel" of the house, the impression of enduring stability, the aura of gracious charm that reminds us of a less hurried and harried age and constitutes, in a very real sense, a secure retreat from the outer world. This effect can be achieved with an old house or a new one, and with furniture that is antique or merely a good copy of one of the traditional styles. In most instances, several of the old styles can be blended harmoniously so that the end result is a feeling of progressive aging that is often even more satisfying than anything accomplished by strict adherence to one period or style. In this book, then, our aim has been to help all those furnishing any Old American style house with Colonial and early post-Colonial furniture and accessories. We have tried to show how modern standards of comfort, charm, and good taste can be attained in houses furnished with antiques or good reproductions of them; how harmony can be achieved between furniture of mixed periods; and the canons of good taste throughout be upheld. And, finally, we have shown how knowledge and judgment may do far more than the mere expenditure of money in securing a home of taste and charm, reflecting the personalities of those who live in it, and owing nothing to fashion's ephemeral whims.

I

YESTERDAY

BACKGROUNDS FOR LIVING: *18th Century architecture today—Relation of house style to interior—How interiors govern furnishing—Principal American architectural styles, 1700–1810 —The furniture periods.*

In the 150 years that have elapsed since the close of the Revolutionary war, life in America has changed tremendously. But, in certain fundamental respects, people's idea of what constitutes a satisfying home has altered very little. In spite of all the scientific and technological developments that have affected home life, we still cling to the 18th century architecture and open fires, and our most treasured possessions are the furniture and furnishings of Colonial days!

And this is as it should be. No other style of American architecture lends itself so well to the small house of today or yesterday, and no other furniture styles so thoroughly complement that architecture in recreating the simple charm of the 18th century home. Today, whether we are the lucky possessors of a house of Colonial vintage; of one built within a score of years after Independence was achieved; or even a good modern copy of either, we can adopt the better designs of furniture produced during the late 17th century and entire 18th century without worrying over problems of taste or suitability. Nor need we question whether we shall grow tired of a style that has endured two centuries or more. In such a Period house we can still have variety, and create within it a home that serves and satisfies us in every way.

Most people want homes that will provide them with the kind of background they desire—a house that reflects their aspirations if not their achievements. But the majority of these houses are shared by several people and compromises are necessary even when the means are available. In spite of all that has been written on the subject, comparatively few people actually are interested in whether or not their home expresses their particular individuality. Self-expression through the furnishing of their homes is not something they consciously seek. Very few indeed would, for example, fill their house with books to impress others with their culture. If their home does happen to reflect their outlook on life and their major interests that is all to the good, but it is not an end in itself, and should not be so.

Actually it does not take long for a house that is really lived in to acquire evidences of the personalities of its owners. If they are simple, home-loving persons, or people inclined to lavish living or display, or are gadabouts who use their house only as a place to be when there is nothing else to do, these characteristics will inevitably reveal themselves in the way the place is furnished, decorated, landscaped, and generally cared for. Furthermore, the interior of the house will reflect their knowledge or ignorance of the fundamental principles of furnishing and of accepted good taste.

One of the most satisfying things about using old-time furniture is the latitude it allows in achieving any special effect, that is, its adaptability. So much of it can be used in any style Colonial house and in combination with pieces of quite different periods. This of course does not mean that one can haphazardly mix all styles of furniture. On the contrary, it is very necessary to be able to discriminate between styles and individual pieces that are harmonious.

You should know exactly why one piece of furniture will seem at home with the rest, or why it will clash and throw the whole room out of key. Given this ability, you can with Colonial furniture, create an impression of almost any degree of formality or informality that you choose. The background and accessories will naturally play a great part in the final result, but first you have to know what pieces to select and how to incorporate them into the general scheme.

While much of this is true in connection with all houses, it has a special application to houses that are closely identified with certain periods in American history. Such Period houses, through their origin and long association, have come to represent in the minds of most some of the more admirable facets of the American character. They are the embodiment in masonry or wood of American life as it was in a day when the middle class and moderately well-to-do citizen—the thriving farmer as well as the small business man of town and village—could build for himself a house that would survive for centuries and, although he did not know it, serve as a monument to that simple sincerity which is the basis of good taste.

This shows how a modern sofa, Queen Anne bonnet-top desk, 18th Century tables, Chippendale and Hepplewhite chairs, Chinese panel, and butler's tray table can form a homogeneous group.

Today, whether through necessity or choice, the majority of American families live in houses whose architectural style was developed during the Colonial period of our history. Most of these houses are copies or adaptations of one or another of the several Colonial and immediately post-Colonial styles and have been built in recent years. The rest are old originals, the majority of which bear all the marks of one and a half to two and a half centuries of living—and too often, we fear, of neglect and mutilation.

If your main interest is with the smaller house—the cottage, the country home of perhaps not more than ten rooms, the converted old-time farm house, the modest old town house, or modern replicas of any of them—you will most likely have but one aim; to invest the interior with quiet comfort and modest charm, while recapturing the spirit of an earlier age that you most admire. Therefore, we can presume that you will be less concerned with dramatic effects, fanciful whimsicalities, or violent contrasts to impress the caller, than achieving what the Old American house can best provide—comfortable living amid attractive surroundings. Upstairs and down, what you will want is rooms that "feel" nice; rooms in which nothing thrusts itself insistently upon your attention—rooms in which you feel comfortable and at ease without knowing why!

Your home is the tangible background of yourself and your family, and perhaps must serve many varied personalities. Therefore it should express no particular dominant mood, even though it can reveal your major preoccupations, pursuits and culture. Everything in that house—the furniture and furnishings and the way they are used and coordinated—should tell the casual visitor but one thing; here lives someone of taste and refinement, though not necessarily of great means. This is the ideal of a great many discerning people, and it is one which the Old American houses and Colonial styles of furniture more than any others can help you to achieve.

The day of furnishing houses with suites of anything is, of course, long gone. Today we assemble groups of individual furniture pieces, and we are thus able to give fuller rein to our imagination, and satisfy our taste. As a result we achieve variety and individuality as never before. Whether we furnish with antiques or reproductions, all that we need to be sure of is that the furniture we acquire is authentic in design, pleasing and unobtrusive in appearance, and suited to our particular style of living. We want furniture and furnishings that seem to "belong." If we have a little old New England farm house, we don't want to cram it full of massive, bulbous Elizabethan furniture or prettify it with classical, frail, and pre-

An old kitchen graciously adapted to modern living with a pine settle, Jacobean gateleg table, 17th Century hanging cupboard, and mushroom ladder-back chair. The Oriental runner is in no wise out of keeping.

tentious Louis XVI creations. We want furniture that is as wholly American Colonial in spirit as the house that contains it. And if we know what
we are doing we can have just that—all without slavishly adhering to
arbitrary rules and decorator's dicta.

With such a home all the normal functions of living can be catered
to in a decent yet practical manner without resort to "practical" modern
innovations—the basement bar, the rumpus room, the breakfast nook or
counter, and meals served alongside the sink. Servantless families can live
as graciously as do those of greater means, albeit on a simpler scale. And
no happier choice of a setting for a harmonious family life than the Old
American style of house could be conceived.

In furnishing such a house, if you have an inborn sense of the fitness
of things and a natural appreciation of what is right and lovely in a home
you are lucky indeed. But even if you are not so fortunate you need not
despair. Furnishing the simple Colonial, or even a Classic Revival style
of house calls for no decorators' tricks, no highly expensive pieces, nor
even quantities of genuine antiques to achieve the results you want.

This is where so many people go wrong. They are told, and they
believe, that the only permissible way to furnish one of these old-time
houses is to reproduce as closely as possible the settings of the day or period
during which the house was built, or of some other selected period during
its history. This is far from being the truth. The major problem is to
secure the old-time flavor, and when you have done that you will discover
that the actual age of each furniture piece—which, incidentally, even
experts might not agree upon—does not matter at all.

You can take a 1740 house and fill it with pieces made in the last
quarter of that century and few will notice the discrepancy. You can even
throw in a few early 19th century accessories and no one but a specialist
would recognize them as being out of keeping. The final test lies in the
skillful choice of pieces, utilitarian, or decorative, that have something in
common. Certain things obviously go together; others clash. Being able
to differentiate is an assurance of success.

Establishing a period atmosphere, then, is something quite different
from restricting the furniture to pieces commonly used together in old-
time houses. There were fashions in those days, too, though they changed
much more slowly than they do today. In refurnishing such a house, therefore, you should aim at recapturing the feel of the rooms rather than
making an exact copy of some specific example from a picture, a dated
restoration, or a museum display.

Informal, Early American type of living room with cork flooring simulating the old wide-board floors. The door from an unused closet to the right of fireplace was removed to allow for recessed bookcase.

Of course it is nice—and useful—to know exactly the items that were commonly included in the various rooms of an old-time house, and that information is readily obtainable. There are plenty of records available on the manner in which houses of different classes were furnished and decorated down to the beginnings of American history. Given a general idea of the furniture and accessories that formed the normal household equipment at any specific period, all we then need to recapture the flavor of that period is a little knowledge of how the basic pieces can inoffensively be combined with others that we consider essential to meet modern standards of comfort, convenience, and efficiency.

But before you make any attempt to furnish an old house, or to decide on the period furniture you would like to use, you need to know two things —the architectural style of the house, and its interior finish. The architecture will be a guide to the period, or period styles you can logically adopt, and the finish will influence the degree of formality in furnishing that you can achieve.

Normally, the architectural style governs the interior details of the house, but these details will vary considerably with the size of the house, and the period during which it was built. If it is a very old house, it may have undergone a process of transition so that the interior no longer bears its original relation to the exterior.

A modern Colonial, likewise, will probably have walls and interior finish that have quite a different appearance and feeling than those of a similar house built 200 years ago. Modern plaster and modern paneling never look quite the same as those that have been mellowed by time; the trim and surfaces are too regular and smooth, and have less character and more formality as a consequence.

All of this has a subtle but nonetheless real effect on the furnished room. The walls, trim, ceiling, and floor constitute the background for your furniture, and may determine whether the final result is pleasing or not. Some of these surfaces can be hidden, disguised, or eliminated but they cannot be ignored. The date at which the house was built, its present condition, and its present interior finish, then, are the first things to be considered in selecting the type of furniture to use. The architectural style of the house, if any, comes next.

In the following discussion of houses and the kinds of furniture that should go in them there is some possibility of confusion unless the system of naming periods is understood. One system is used for furniture and another for houses, and the same term may mean two different things.

Houses are assigned to periods according to their style and regardless of when they were built. The three major styles of houses dealt with here are: (1) the Early American, (2) Georgian, (3) the Greek Revival. The Early Americans, built since the 17th century, are of two general types— the Northern and the Southern. The Northern Early American is a central chimney style of house of 1, 1½, 2, or even 3 stories height. It has no hall but a tiny entry at the front of the chimney from which a stair rises to the second floor. Special types of Early Americans are the Cape Cod (1½ story), and the saltbox which has the roof coming down to the first floor level at the back.

The Southern Early American has either one or two chimneys—one in each gable end. Usually it has a small entry at the center but no hallway. In the very small houses the outside door may open into one of the rooms. Those built in the north were more likely to be of wood while those in the south were more often of brick. Room arrangements varied accordingly, but informality was the keynote in both.

The Georgian houses, built from 1720 on, were usually somewhat larger and more spacious than the Early Americans, and much more impressive and formal both inside and out. With two chimneys (the larger ones had four), they had fireplaces in four to eight rooms, central halls, and featured the staircases. An equivalent house in the Southern colonies may have had an exterior of brick but the interior finish would be somewhat similar. There would be varying proportions of wooden wall surfaces, but the general air of the structure would be slightly more formal than in the case of the New England house. Often the Georgian houses have hipped roofs instead of the ridge roof of the Early Americans. They also have a high foundation and a central hall giving access to all ground floor rooms.

The Greek Revival houses are a classical style developed in post-Revolutionary days, adorned with heavy porch columns and pedimented gables so that they look more like Greek temples than homes. The main entrance is usually in a gable, but the external shape and internal room arrangements vary a great deal. Few of these houses were built after 1830 or so except in the Western Reserve (Ohio), but Georgians and Early Americans are standard types today.

The Early Americans, North and South, the Georgian and Greek Revival, then, were the major styles of houses built before the Victorian era and are still copied in modified form today. But a great many houses were also built between 1700 and 1830 that cannot strictly be classified as belonging to one of these styles. These were the nondescripts, the products of provincial and country carpenters and builders. And many of them made quite satisfactory dwellings as, with a few modifications, they still do.

So much for the house periods. When we speak of furniture periods we use a different system. The earliest furniture made in this country by the Massachusetts colonists is called Pilgrim furniture, or, more properly, Early Colonial. The name Early American is reserved for furniture also known as American Provincial or kitchen furniture, made in country districts after the Revolution.

The rest of the furniture made here takes its name from the English furniture from which it was copied, such as Jacobean, Carolean, William-and-Mary, Queen Anne. Early Georgian was a development of the Queen Anne style, lasting till the time of Chippendale and the coming into fashion of mahogany furniture.

Furniture of the middle and late Georgian eras is really the middle and late forms of Chippendale. The late Georgian also includes the work of Hepplewhite, Adam, and Sheraton which lasted through the Revolution. The middle period saw the rise of many important American furniture designers and makers, but few have become lastingly famous. Names like Savery and Goddard were overshadowed by the originator of the furniture they copied—Chippendale—except in their own neighborhoods, until the 20th century when their work was rediscovered and their fame revived. After the Revolution the greatest name in American furniture was Phyfe whose classic style finally degenerated into the less-desirable late Empire.

Theoretically, each of these styles of houses called for its own particular brand of furniture, but, as we have indicated, the furnishing possibilities actually are governed just as much by the interior finish and style as by the architecture of the house.

2

THE COLONIAL HOUSE: *Characteristics of Early American houses—Authentic interiors—Progressive developments—The factor of room size—Georgian and Greek Revival interiors—Accommodating modern innovations—Choosing the furniture style.*

If the house you are proposing to furnish is a very early Early American, the rooms will be quite small, many of the structural timbers will be exposed, and there will be a great deal of unpainted woodwork, such as board sheathing, board walls, and even paneling. In the 17th century houses there may be little or no plaster. By 1700 however the woodwork in the houses was considerably reduced and plaster walls were becoming common. The woodwork, nevertheless, continued bare and the walls were either untouched plaster or whitewashed. Twenty-five years later, those householders who could afford it—or spare the time to make it—had succumbed to the use of paint. They covered up the woodwork of the old houses, and painted the woodwork of the new ones.

This use of paint for interiors gave carpenters an excuse for using wood of poorer grades, such as pine marred by a rash of dark knots. Since the wood surface was hidden under the paint there could be no complaint. This was all right until the 20th century pine enthusiasts came along and ruthlessly removed the paint. Today we find a great many pine interiors that should never have been robbed of their paint coatings. We also find, as a direct result of this, lumber dealers advertising and advocating "knotty pine" for everything from furniture to wall boarding. A gullible public accepts this because they think knotty pine is authentic and has an antique air. Actually it has neither, and to those who know, it is also offensive to the eye. Therefore we do not encourage the adoption, old or new, of knotty pine backgrounds for old-time rooms. Where these are present, they should be painted over or removed. Much better results from every standpoint will be secured with clear pine properly antiqued.

The authentic Early American interior, then, will be of clear, unpainted pine, perhaps oak, (or some other wood having a similar tone and appearance); of natural plaster walls, or plaster whitened; of exposed girts, beams, and joists; of unpainted wood trim around windows, and doors; and plank floors of oak or pine. After 1727 or so we may rightly expect that some of the interior woodwork will be painted.

The vogue for painted woodwork increased as the century grew older, and even in the poorer houses colored walls were found. The lack of good lumber, or the higher cost of labor, may have forced the use of cased-in timbers, which made little difference when the surfaces were painted. Then, around 1750, wallpapers, though expensive, were sometimes used in the smaller houses, though most had to be contented with painted decorations such as stencil work. A little before 1800 when commercial paints were obtainable at reasonable prices, painted and decorated floors, especially in the best rooms, grew in popularity. The well-known spatter-dash treatment, however, rarely occurred before 1840.

These were the major changes in interior treatments of the Early American houses between 1700 and the early 1800s. And this progressive development might well have happened to any one house. A house built in 1700 might conceivably have originally had boarded or paneled walls, and exposed timbers. As time went on, part of the woodwork may have been replaced by plaster, and still later the timbers encased or covered by a plaster ceiling; wainscots cut down to chair-rail height, and so on. Floors once covered with a sprinkling of sand may have been first oiled, and later painted.

The exterior of the house may not have changed at all, but most likely more or larger windows have been installed, blinds added or removed, and extensions tacked onto the original building. Many houses grew by additions throughout the 18th century and today one part may be 50 to 150 years older than the rest.

And so the old house kept pace with the changing times. Yet to us, 150 years later, that house still is an antique, with the mellow charm that well-preserved old age brings. As a result when we come to furnish it we are faced with the problem of what period in its history to choose. Logically we should furnish in the style corresponding to the latest changes in the interior. But if we actually have a house built in the early 1700s we may not want to "decorate" it in an 1800 dress. A house of the Revolutionary period would likewise not be suitably furnished with pieces dating from the 17th century. This is one aspect of the furnishing problem.

Example of a formal Georgian entrance hall, with black and white tiled floor. The tiles are of a composition simulating marble.

Another, and one which, it seems to us, is often of more cogency in determining the treatment, is the size of the rooms. With these small houses it is usually the case that the earlier the date, the lower the ceilings, and the tinier the rooms. Practically, there is little that can be done about room height. Sometimes the ceilings are removed, exposing beams and joists that were never meant to be exposed. This gives more air space which helps those with claustrophobic tendencies, but removes no hazards to tall people, and usually spoils the room. Removing walls or partitions is simpler and a common solution for floor space problems, even though it may take away the intimate charm of the rooms, and destroy the authentic air of the house. That of course is a penalty of "progress" which calls for the sacrifice of sentiment to expediency. If, in our small Early American houses, we can retain the tiny rooms, we shall have a good start in recapturing the flavor of an earlier age when we come to arrange our *lares et penates.*

Georgian and Greek Revival Interiors

Much of what has been said in connection with the Early American house also applies to the Georgian houses. This style of house is intrinsically more dignified and elaborate than the Early American. It was usually mounted on a high foundation, so that, unlike the Early American which hugged the ground, it reached an imposing height.

Inside, the wooden trim of the rooms was more elaborate, cupboards were built in, and even to the end of the Colonial Period and after, the houses continued to be built with impressive paneling in the principal rooms, upstairs and down. Intricate moldings were used around the windows and doors and fireplace mantels. Much of the time this woodwork was painted.

The structural members, from the mid-century on, were almost always hidden in walls and ceilings. Exposed timbers were considered primitive by then.

The Greek Revival type of architecture called for interiors along the general lines of the very late Georgian houses. The principal difference was that the moldings were less fancy and more severely classical in their decorations. On the other hand, the very small houses of this style were often much plainer, and the sizes and proportions of the rooms were the principal points of distinction.

Like all other styles of house, the Greek Revivals varied in detail. They often had tall windows coming almost to the floor, as did some of the late Georgians, and the expansive Palladian windows of the Georgians were even put in Greek Revival gables. Both types of house lent themselves very well to imposing entrance halls. But apart from such details, it is the "feel" of all these houses that matters most in furnishing them. And that "feel" which is governed by the exterior impressiveness, the quality of the interior finish of the bare rooms, and the proportions of those rooms, is something you cannot readily mistake.

Just as you can detect quality in people the moment you meet them and talk with them, so are you able to sense the degree of refinement of the house when you mentally note its characteristics inside and out. And that appreciation is what should rightfully determine your approach to the problems of satisfactorily furnishing your Old American house.

Factors in Furnishing

From the foregoing brief incursion into backgrounds it will have been gathered that there is more to deciding upon a suitable furnishing scheme than the date and type of the house, or even your preconceived notions of what you like and dislike in an old-time house adapted to modern living.

In furnishing any old house that is to be lived in in the 20th century style, you have to allow for modern innovations. It is hard to imagine living the year round in a house without electric lighting, a telephone, radio, full bookcases, overstuffed furniture, suitable floor coverings, up-to-date kitchen and bathroom equipment, heating appurtenances such as radiators or grilles, and so forth. Normally, these things will detract from the old time flavor of a room, yet they must be made to blend unobtrusively with the furniture and furnishings of another age. Fortunately, in most instances, that can be done to a satisfactory degree.

In nine cases out of ten, then, the whole problem consists of creating an authentic background, and tastefully arranging against it furniture of the proper styles and vintages combined with modern pieces and equipment so treated that they harmonize with the furniture and add to rather than detract from the old-time flavor. Admittedly, this is usually a great deal harder to do successfully than it is to describe. There are often complications.

Since so many of us acquire odd pieces of furniture from time to time, our furnishing plans may have become involved. There is the problem of how to incorporate these objects—some antique, some just old, some lovely, and some plain ghastly—into our well-planned house. That problem will seem simpler when you have studied the old furniture styles and attributes and learned what looks well with what, and why.

One thing you do not have to fear in furnishing with this old furniture is standardization. We have seen a great many houses furnished in Colonial style, but we have yet to encounter any two that are even remotely alike in general appearance or actual arrangement. Individuality seems to be something that is hard to suppress when an interested and knowledgeable owner furnishes his or her own home. In this, of course, accessories play a great part, as do colors and background materials. This is the reason why selecting the principal furniture period is only the beginning of furnishing.

Another important factor is the objective you have in mind in furnishing your home in any particular style. You may adore the masculinity of William-and-Mary, or delight in the delicate fragility of Hepplewhite. But it will, as a rule, pay you to reserve final decision till you have considered the furniture in relation to your house. You may then come to decide that you will get more lasting satisfaction by concentrating on recapturing the old-time atmosphere, mellow and gracious, that the style of house you live in suggests.

It may be surprising to discover that this does not necessarily mean furnishing a house built in 1700 with nothing but the kind of furniture you would expect to buy in that remote year. For one thing you would soon learn that there never existed in America sufficient articles of 17th century furniture to equip the small house for anything approximating even 18th century living. The houses of the 17th century that were occupied by people of average means were not provided with anything but the barest necessities, and most comfort according to present day standards was totally lacking. Seats were benches, settles, or stools, and often the head of the family was the only one to attain the dignity of using a board-seated chair.

This being so, you would be forced to consider the use of some furniture pieces of later dates, and immediately you would lose the strict authenticity you were seeking. On the other hand, since you are primarily putting together a home and not a museum display, this is not of so great importance as it may have seemed.

Actually, what most owners of old houses really want is not a strict reproduction of a group of Period rooms. They simply want to get into each room some of the grace and serenity they would expect to find in one that had been assembled and cared for by generations of home-loving people; a room permeated with a feeling of continuity and stability in a world of change, that fills its occupants with a sense of well-being and satisfaction because of its comfort and charm. This calls for rooms that are in keeping with the rest of the house and look as though they had belonged there a long, long time.

Of course even in mixing your Periods, you may be creating an authentic interior because that is usually what happened to the old houses during their long life. In the beginning, the majority of very early houses had nothing distinctive about them, and today we should not be satisfied to live in them. Many an early room possessed one imposing piece of furniture and little else. Luckily the room grew in convenience and comfort as time went on and new pieces of furniture and fresh arrangements were introduced, interior finishes improved, and up-to-date accessories added. And so through the years, they acquired real character and an air of permanency that increased with the passage of time.

In some cases it is to be expected that drastic changes were made from time to time in the furnishing. New pieces were added and old ones eliminated, or a complete change in style adopted. Houses whose rooms were informal in the beginning may gradually have taken on a more dignified air through changes in interior finishes to blend with more formal furniture that the rising fortunes of the family or popular fashion dictated.

At any rate, more often than not, any old house by the late 18th century would, most likely, be furnished with a variety of pieces over a period of several generations. Good furniture was expensive in those days and not lightly discarded.

In the usual course of things, people acquire the house they are going to live in before they get the furniture to equip it. On the other hand, many of us "make do" for a few years with a variety of furniture pieces we have acquired or inherited, or we collect one or two special antiques we would like to build our home around. We must, of course, know enough to decide which of these we can use as they are, which can be sufficiently transformed or adapted by being made over, painted, or decorated, and which must forever be relegated to the attic or the junk pile. And it is for just that reason that we require a combination of knowledge and good taste. Books can give us the knowledge, but taste must be cultivated by studying what people of acknowledged good taste do, and analyzing the reasons for ourselves.

Ordinarily, it is simpler, cheaper, and generally more satisfactory to adapt our furniture to the house than vice versa. At least we have much more scope for achieving interesting rooms without having to work odd pieces into a general scheme in which they do not naturally belong. Apart from this, as we have already hinted, the average Colonial house, antique or not, will afford an appropriate background or setting for a wide range of old American furniture styles. The kind of house that has been in use for a couple of hundred years will, unless it has been extensively mis-handled, accommodate itself nicely to more than one of the old furniture styles that were developed throughout that period.

We do of course have to limit our choice of styles to periods after the earliest date at which our type of house was first used. And we do have to consider the degree of formality, or informality, the house demands. With these facts in mind, then, we can turn our attention to the furnishing of our own Old American house, starting out by deciding what type of house it is that we have—formal or informal, new or old, early in feeling or late.

3

ADAPTING THE HOUSE: *Fitting house to furniture—How to add or decrease formality—Ways of making small houses look big, and vice-versa—Comparisons of interiors—Small rooms vs. big ones —Colors for interiors.*

The furniture we are going to talk about is intended for use in houses —not mansions. Those houses, presumably will be, or are, in existence before the furniture is chosen. Therefore since the houses will determine the suitability or otherwise of the things that go into them, it will pay us to examine their merits and limitations before we consider the furniture.

Fitting House to Furniture

Regardless of whether your tastes are inclined to formal or informal furnishing, your house itself will have an important influence on the final result. On the other hand, there are a great many things you can do to counteract some of the features of a house that determine character. Size, for instance, is important. But even the apparent size (or smallness) of a house can be changed, so far as the eye is concerned. The smaller the house the less formal you would expect it to be. But the impression of smallness, the cottage air, can be counteracted in a number of ways. The house won't be any larger, but it may seem so, and it is the impression that counts. A cottage atmosphere is contributed by several things—the way the house nestles on the ground and into its surroundings; the formality of its trim; and its colorings are the three most important. Your "ivy covered cottage" or your northern Early American type of old Colonial can be given a slightly more formal air by surrounding it with geometrically laid out lawns and flower beds, and by using plants, flowers, and shrubs that are not so obviously old-timey as hollyhocks, and lilac bushes, or rambler roses. Staked dahlias, day lilies, and delphiniums are examples of the more sophisticated looking plants, as are clipped hedges of almost any kind.

Fencing the garden with something more formal than pointed pickets, such as a railing finished with molding, also is a big help. The house can be given a slightly high-hat air by adding a "Tory chimney"—that is, by painting it white with a black top. Often the house itself can be formalized by replacing an old stone step with brick, and perhaps mounting an iron hand rail on it. This, of course, is more of a Georgian feature than an Early American one, but it is often found on both clapboard and brick town houses of the central-chimney type. The ultimate in formality is reached when a Colonial brass knocker is added to a neatly painted and paneled door. Knobs of course are more formal than latches.

Logic suggests that a small house painted white will be more formal in appearance than one painted barn red. But actually this is rarely so. The red houses may be barn color, but with the corner boards and trim painted white or gray, as they usually are, they look so neat and so primly tidy that they lose the casual cottage feel. This seems to apply to the same houses painted gray and white or even those colored tan or yellow and some other trim color. It is the contrasting trim that does the trick, drawing straight line borders around the main structure. A somewhat similar effect is produced when a brick house is painted white. Extra formality is added when the landscaping is horizontal and unbroken, and when brick or tile terraces are used.

Most Georgian houses have many of these features, but when they have lost some of their dignity through neglect or changes in the externals, the remedy is obvious. Reducing the formal feel of a small Georgian type house often merely means raising the foundation plantings; the apparent height of the building is cut down by raising the garden beds near the walls. This is done by adding soil and sloping the beds, or raising them with stone borders. If the lawn can be sloped up to the top of the foundation so much the better. The rest is a matter of planting.

The very small house can be made more important looking by being raised above the surroundings. A lawn sloping up to the house is apt to make the house look higher than if the ground sloped down. Tall trees reduce the apparent size of the house and vice versa. A high, boxy little house needs its horizontal lines exaggerated to give it better proportions. You could do this by increasing the apparent width of the windows with colored blinds, by painting the window trim a different color than the walls, by installing a more imposing, and wider entrance, by flanking the front

Early American style living room furnished with adaptations of provincial pieces in maple suited to the simple country home.

door with side lights, by lowering high windows, by reducing the height of the chimney or making it fatter, by extending the eaves down over the front a few inches, by putting long eyebrow windows in a 1½ story wall, by tacking a horizontal trellis along the front wall above the lower or upper windows, and trailing a vine along it.

If none of these treatments of the house itself does the trick, you can extend the house by adding a porch or pergola-roofed terrace to either or both gables; or by extending the foundation line with a roofless terrace or a low wall. Where you have a setback extension of the main house, you can sometimes add a porch roof over the space in front of it to reveal the full length of the building. These and a number of other dodges can be used to change the external appearance of the house so that it conforms better to the degree of formality of the interior.

Inside the house also there are a few things you can do to obtain similar results. But whether you propose to change the character of the interior or the exterior, it is well not to lose sight of the fact that authenticity is also important. You do not want a freakish house that is neither fish, flesh, nor fowl, nor good red herring. When you are through, the house should still be recognized for what it originally was, otherwise it will lose more than it gains by the transformation.

A thoroughly informal old house cannot satisfactorily be made over into an utterly formal one without losing a great deal of its original appeal. With a modern house, of course, you can go a great deal further because you have not so much of that intangible air to lose. Within certain limitations, however, you can adapt your old house to various degrees of formality. The important thing is to know where to stop.

This understanding is particularly important in connection with the interior. We have seen utterly informal cottage-type houses made absurd by "paneling" the plaster walls with frames of molding, and dressed up by planing all the character out of the old floor boards.

Without going to such lengths, some of the things you *can* do to increase the formality of a simple interior are: use a dressy color of paint for the woodwork; use more formal fireplace mantels; tint the plaster walls; apply plaster moldings in the angle between wall and ceiling; use paneled doors in place of the batten type; use smooth plaster instead of the rough, sand finished kind; use semi-formal wallpaper, and expensive looking lighting fixtures; have uneven hearthstones and floors leveled; use tiles instead of plaster around the fireplace openings, or "marble" the plaster with paint.

Attractive example of the informal living room furnished with Early American adaptations. While the squared wallpaper and squared upholstery might be questioned, the curtain fabric and braided rug are good.

An informal Early American atmosphere achieved in a modern hall with linoleum cork flooring, stencilled wall, reproduction lighting fixture, and hooked rug of excellent design. Note decorated chest.

You can install ornate baseboards and other decorative moldings in rooms that have plain ones; and even add built-in cupboards of antique design. Primitive styles of hardware may also be replaced with later styles, preferably of brass. Even if such background changes do not entirely provide the atmosphere that is sought, they will go a long way toward making the furniture and accessories seem at home.

If you are dealing with a larger house and want to detract from the too-dignified air, you can reverse some of these processes, but your greatest difficulty will be in making a large room look informal without its furniture. Other things being equal, you will find that unpainted woodwork that is not highly finished looks much less formal than painted wood. Paneling, of course, is more formal in feel than boarding or sheathing, and plain boards (even of the feather-edged type) are less dressy than boards decorated with a bead or molding. Door trim, especially, affects the general impression a room gives.

In a cottage type house, the trim is usually plain and flat, with perhaps a simple bead along the inner edge. The top rail usually extends across the top of the stiles. The use of molding around the door opening, with mitred corners like a picture frame, is much more fancy. Molded stiles, with applied rosettes at the top, are about the limit to which you can go in adorning the plain farmhouse interior trim.

Pedimented doors are best reserved for spacious Georgian rooms. Wide floor boards for some reason look more primitive than narrower ones, and random lengths than equal ones. Oak floors are somewhat more formal than pine ones in the same condition, and painted floors than oiled ones.

If you have a large kitchen fireplace with a bake oven at the side, you can tone down its crudity in several ways. In many such fireplaces, the door over the oven and the opening beneath it, is missing. Replacing the door gives a much tidier appearance. Using a paneled door instead of a batten type adds dignity. A spring catch likewise is less crude than a wood turn-button. Blackening the brick around the fireplace opening dresses up the old fireplaces, and in some instances, whitewashing the stone cheeks has the same effect. A castiron fireback also helps.

Bedroom fireplace openings that are too large and inclined to smoke, can be both dressed up and helped by adding a raised back hearth. A layer of bricks on the bottom of the fireplace does this, and the outer hearthstone also can be covered with bricks held in place by a thick wooden frame. Such hearths are occasionally found in very old houses so there is plenty of precedent for them.

In Georgian houses that have too-large rooms for your style of furnishing, you can often make the rooms smaller and add much-needed closets at the same time. In the small houses it is common practice to remove or change the location of partitions and walls. On old houses of some historic value, this of course borders on vandalism. But where it is absolutely necessary, such changes serve to add formality and widen your scope for furnishing attractively, particularly where there are few unbroken wall spaces and too many doors.

The slight variations in the degree of formality that are affected by the foregoing adjustments and alterations are often all that is needed to give the refinished interior an agreeable air of unity. That effect is something that is more often than not achieved apparently accidentally. At least it frequently happens that of two rooms similarly furnished, one will have that touch that makes all the difference. And that touch may well be some detail of the background that seems a very little and unimportant thing in itself.

Interior finish, and harmony with the exterior, then, are the first steps in furnishing the Colonial house. Authenticity in texture and in finish of the surfaces, in the kinds of moldings used, and the colors applied are essential parts of this step. In the very old houses there usually are original moldings that can be copied. Otherwise it is necessary to refer to an expert or some authoritative book on the subject.

As regards colors, one simple source is the material put out in connection with authentic Williamsburg paints. These range from mellow ivory through Colonial blue to dusky red. Primitive houses can use the commoner Indian red or buttermilk blue, and several shades of gray as well. This matter of color is discussed in greater detail in the chapter on wall coverings. But the foregoing is sufficient to indicate the wide range of possibilities in furnishing almost any kind of Old American house.

4

STYLES, PERIODS, AND PIECES: *Traditional style charac-*
teristics—Formal vs. informal pieces—Style compatibility—Distin-
guishing features—Early Colonial style—Pilgrim interiors—Enter
William-and-Mary.

In order to be able to select the right kind of furniture you need to
know something about the traditional styles and the characteristics by which
you can identify them. You also need to understand the features that determine whether or not a piece is formal or informal in appearance and why.
Beyond that point, judgment is largely a matter of taste. There are, however, a number of generally accepted notions that form a valuable guide to
furniture selection.

Some of the points to consider, on which most of us need no reminders,
concern the suitability of the pieces to one another and to the room. The
size and the impression of massiveness or lightness that design gives to certain pieces is usually something that we can feel without taking a tape measure to them. For instance, tables or chairs that are underbraced always look
heavier than similar pieces without the bracing. Pierced or cutout (*à jour*)
surfaces seem, and often are, lighter than solid ones, straight, square legs
sit more solidly than tapered or curved ones, and so on.

Similarly, if we cannot always gauge the "feel" of furniture we may
be instinctively aware that oak is not as formal as mahogany, and inlaid
pieces are richer in effect than plain ones. These facts will no doubt become
apparent when we compare the various furniture styles that were in vogue
during the Colonial Period in America. But in making such comparisons we
need to see the furniture itself. Photographs, drawings, or pictures of any
kind which reproduce the outlines and form in a small scale are deceptive
in this respect.

In discussing the furniture it is hardly necessary to go into detail on the lives and work of the designers and makers responsible for the Colonial styles. It should be sufficient to date the periods and examine the salient features of each furniture style. This will enable us to classify the styles as to general characteristics and compatibility one with the other. With this information anyone can readily tell what styles and pieces can successfully be used together and which of them can be relied upon to provide the effect desired.

The only way in which you can learn to distinguish one style from another when you see them is to familiarize yourself with the general appearance and principal features of each, and note the details in which they differ. This means comparing either pictures or examples of one with those of another, noting their differences as well as their likenesses.

Of course not everyone wants to become an expert on furniture history, and if you want to know just enough to be able to make intelligent decisions in furnishing your own home you can be satisfied with learning to generalize broadly. Usually what happens then is that the subject becomes too fascinating to drop at that point, or you get to discussing the subject with friends, and are astonished and sometimes embarrassed, to find that they speak with more authority than you. And that, of course, is an intolerable situation you do your best to remedy.

Be this as it may, you cannot talk about or even read of the various furniture styles and the periods to which they belong without having some sort of mental picture of the various pieces. When you are actually furnishing a home of course you need to know much more. You have to be able to visualize what groups or single pieces of some particular style will look like in a room. And you need to be able to decide what kinds of furniture go together and why some of them seem out of place.

Since most of us have to furnish rooms in our mind's eye before we actually buy the pieces, we need to know exactly what we are doing when we select one piece instead of another. In this connection it is perhaps fortunate that most of the furniture styles adopted and developed in Colonial America bore some relation to one another. Furthermore, there was for the most part no violent transition from one to the other. Styles overlapped and there were many points of resemblance between them, particularly in the transitional stage. This helps when we need to mix our periods but adds to the difficulty of identifying the styles.

And so familiarity is the only answer—you must get to know each style at first hand: Visit the museums or inspect private collections, and examine in detail pieces that have already been identified as to style and date. If you are going to spend a great deal of money on furnishing your home and buying things that will be a part of your life for many years to come, that is the least precaution you can take. Meanwhile you can make a start by learning the dates and sequences of the furniture periods and the styles associated with them. Here we can only review the highlights.

In furnishing your Old American house, then, it may be comforting to know that you may have the choice of around ten different styles of Colonial and Early American furniture. And luckily several of these can be combined in a manner that will produce pleasing results in formal, semi-formal, and informal rooms. In addition to the traditional styles of English or Dutch origin and informal pieces made here, there is one other foreign style it will be advantageous to include. The 18th century French Provincial style, once so popular in the French settlements of the colonies, blends so well with certain types of Colonial furniture that it cannot be excluded from any halfway complete survey of Colonial furnishing styles.

The principal periods with which Colonial furniture styles are identified, dating from the 1600s to the beginning of the 19th century, are somewhat as follows.

Early Colonial

In the early 1600s the colonists copied the designs of various pieces of furniture with which they had been familiar in England and Holland. Since the Puritan fathers frowned upon display and frivolity the carpenters cooperated by eliminating any decoration or embellishment there may have been on the original pieces they copied. The results were strictly utilitarian.

This furniture was first made in oak, then in the more tractable and readily obtainable woods such as ash, pine, and, later, maple. These pieces however were not sufficiently diversified to constitute a furniture style. Nevertheless the individual pieces are referred to as Pilgrim or Early Colonial to distinguish them from the imported pieces and those that came after.

At this time a few pieces of Elizabethan furniture were imported—a massive style, best suited to baronial halls, that had persisted in England since the late 16th century. The Elizabethan had already been largely superseded in England by the Early Jacobean, a somewhat lighter and less ornamented version of the Tudor Elizabethan.

A little later, the English Revolution of 1649 brought about a modification of the Early Jacobean. The furniture was stripped of its decorative features. The style became plain and austere in appearance as befitted Cromwell and his Roundheads, and no doubt suited the New England Puritans

One of the first slat-back chairs. Called a "mushroom" chair because of the flattened tops of the front leg posts.

precisely. This short period of 1649 to 1660 gave the name Cromwellian to this severe Jacobean style, but not much is seen or heard of it these days.

The late Jacobean style of furniture was that developed during the Restoration of England's Stuart kings, and is therefore sometimes called the Stuart style—with little apparent reason beyond confusing the student. French influence introduced a taste for luxury that is expressed in the sumptuous decoration of this furniture.

It was during the latter part of this period that walnut began to take the place of oak, much of it decorated with beautiful carving to which walnut so well lends itself. The oppressive influence of the Puritans was dying away.

Pilgrim Interiors

In the earliest New England days comfort was unthought of and at least outwardly despised by the Puritans and Pilgrims. Their inadequate houses had very little furniture at all and what they had was confined to bare essentials. It is true they had some simple, but very lovely, chests—long boxes standing 20 to 30 inches high. Some of these chests the immigrants had brought with them; others were made after they arrived. Those made here were for the most part of plain pine boards, perhaps with some simple design or the owner's initials carved on the front. Some had feet formed by extending the end boards downward a few inches, but many did not.

The chests that were brought from the homeland were practically always of oak, and sometimes carved all over. Before long the New England joiners and arkwrights were making chests with a drawer below. Then came chests with several drawers, and from that they went to chests mounted on legs, perhaps beautifully carved, or painted, or both. But for a long time these low chests served many purposes—as seats, tables, and even beds!

The second important item of furniture in these early Puritan homes was the bed. The less well-off slept on pallets on the floor. Others who could afford the time and had the skill made themselves a one-post bed. This had only one leg, two sides being fastened to the walls. Going to the other extreme, some beds, called press beds, had six legs and a hinge so that they could be folded up when not in use. Space was at a premium in these tiny houses.

By the middle of the 17th century, however, the majority of New England's population had comparatively well-furnished homes. At least they had a choice of tables—the hutch type, which also served as a small chest or even a seat; trestles, which could be taken apart after every meal for the same space-saving reason. If space was not so important they could use permanently assembled stretcher, sawbuck, or refectory tables. A little later—around 1680—someone in Connecticut came up with a small butterfly table, so beloved of antique collectors today. Meanwhile new arrivals of more than average means brought in some gateleg tables of Jacobean design.

Chairs were scarce items in the beginning. Often only the head of the house was accorded the dignity of a seat to himself at table. The rest of the family sat on long forms (benches) or pulled up backless joint stools. The first chairs were massive affairs called wainscot chairs. They had flat, straight backs of solid or panelled wood, and flat wood seats. Some self-indulgent Puritan no doubt interposed a cushion of sorts between himself and the uncompromising boards, but history does not record such indulgence as common.

An early Governor of Massachusetts named Carver brought a chair to New England with him and thereby achieved immortality. The Carver chair is well-known and much admired today. This and a somewhat similar chair introduced by a certain Deacon (or Elder) Brewster, was made of turned wood, principally oak and ash. The Carver chair was the less Spartan of the two, having a rush seat, and quite a few less turned spindles.

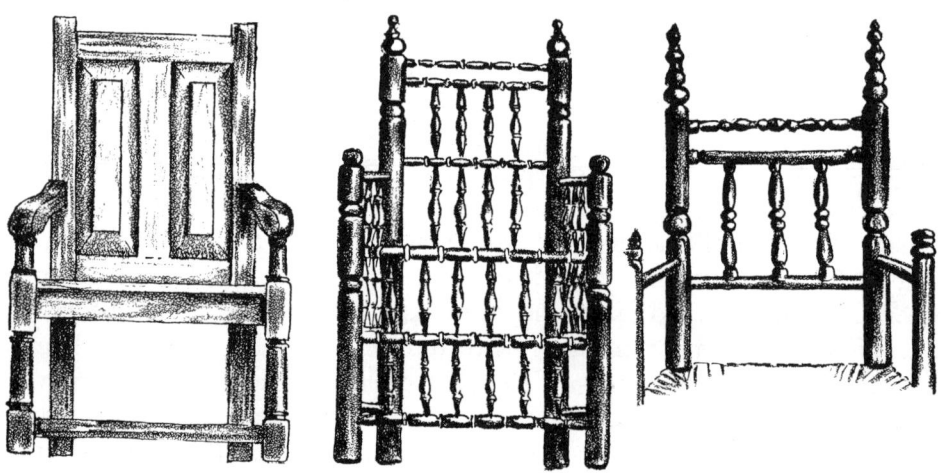

The three earliest American chair styles—Wainscot, Brewster, Carver.

The Pilgrims are credited with developing, from a less inspired Elizabethan product, a slat-back chair with a rush seat and curiously shaped tops to the front legposts. These flat, round finials earned them the name of mushroom chairs. Incidentally, one of the most beautiful chairs ever designed was made in northern New England in the 1790s. It is a turned spindle type with three slats and a rush seat. The spindles are marvels of design, and the slats are reminiscent of angel's wings. It is called the Salamander chair from the outline of the slats which are supposed to look like a

Late William-and-Mary style wing chair with X-braced, trumpet-turned legs—one of the first wing chairs.

pair of salamanders, nose to nose! The design of the chair is said to date from Francis I of France whose emblem was the salamander.

The high-backed armchairs with three slats were soon followed by side chairs with two slats and somewhat lower backs. These were soon so common that women, and even children, finally achieved the distinction of a seat to themselves at meals.

Other seats of the Pilgrim period were fireside settles of pine which could be moved around as desired. Well-to-do families may also have had such fancy pieces as a day-bed. This was practically the same thing as a modern *chaise longue,* with six or eight legs, a leather or cane back, and a loose cushion. But the dream of every housewife undoubtedly was for a fancy cupboard of which there were several particularly desirable styles.

One type was the court cupboard and another the press cupboard. Those known as livery cupboards, which were used for storing food, were apparently much rarer in northern latitudes. At any rate very few have survived to this day. The most that many of the old-time housekeepers would acquire would be a so-called "hutch"—a cupboard on legs in which to keep her cups and trenchers.

So much for New England. Now let us see what the colonists in the South were doing for furniture at this time. History tells us that while the Puritans and the Pilgrims were busy settling New England (hitherto known

Modern reproductions of the "four-back" side and arm chair.

as Northern Virginia), a very different type of pioneer was carving a home out of the southern Virginia wilderness. These southern colonists as a whole, were a wealthier and a better educated class than their northern neighbors. They had money, servants, and good connections in the old country. Hence they were able to live on a more luxurious scale from the beginning.

They got substantial houses built in the early 1600s and sent home for furniture they had not been able to bring with them. Those who came after 1630 or so brought along many comforts. They had great Elizabethan oak bedsteads, plenty of court, press, and livery cupboards of massive construction, and tall floor cupboards. For seats they had a variety of chairs with loose cushions, stools, forms, and several kinds of tables and buffets.

Well before the end of the century they had imported Jacobean oak and walnut furniture and were copying or adapting that style to their own colonial taste. That taste was far more formal than in the Puritan North.

Unlike that of either North or South was the furniture of the Dutch inhabiting what is now New York. In the 17th century they were enjoying

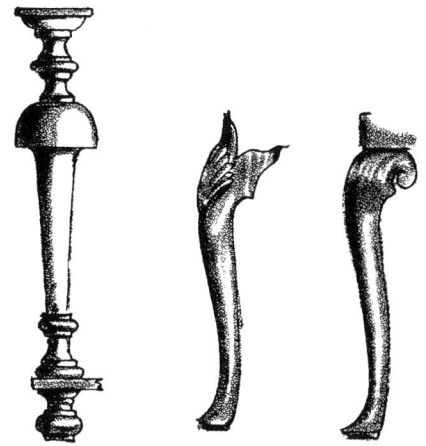

The William-and-Mary inverted cup leg (left) and two styles of the early Queen Anne cabriole leg, one with leaf decoration, one without.

the furniture styles then current in Holland. Much of their furniture was made with turned spindles with a characteristic fat bulbous portion in the center. The Dutch also used Flemish chairs which had a great deal of carving, and caned seats and back. The influence of Spain was revealed in the chair feet which were of the style known to us as the Spanish foot.

The Dutch also had very heavy oak presses on ball, turnip, or onion feet, with deep panels and wide, heavy moldings. They also had a standing cupboard called a kas, which might have a plain surface painted in elaborate designs or have applied decorations, such as diamond-shaped pieces of wood nailed to it.

Enter William-and-Mary

The next great furniture period to influence Colonial styles was that named after the Dutch king of England, William of Orange, and his English Queen, Mary, daughter of James II. This period (1689–1702), called William-and-Mary, marked the introduction of a new furniture style, largely Dutch in origin, which was lighter and more graceful than the Jacobean, and comparatively comfortable. However it was still somewhat large in scale and strongly constructed, the heavy pieces having their legs braced together with curved or X-shaped stretchers. The legs themselves were mostly turnings in the trumpet, pegtop, or inverted cup forms, with flattened ball (bun) feet. Another form of leg was the S-shaped or Flemish scroll type, and, later on, the bandy or cabriole form with or without a shell carving on the knee.

William-and-Mary cabinets were made with a double arched (hooded) top. There were also tall clocks of inlaid walnut, and square-topped dressing tables with multi-arched aprons. This was the period during which the

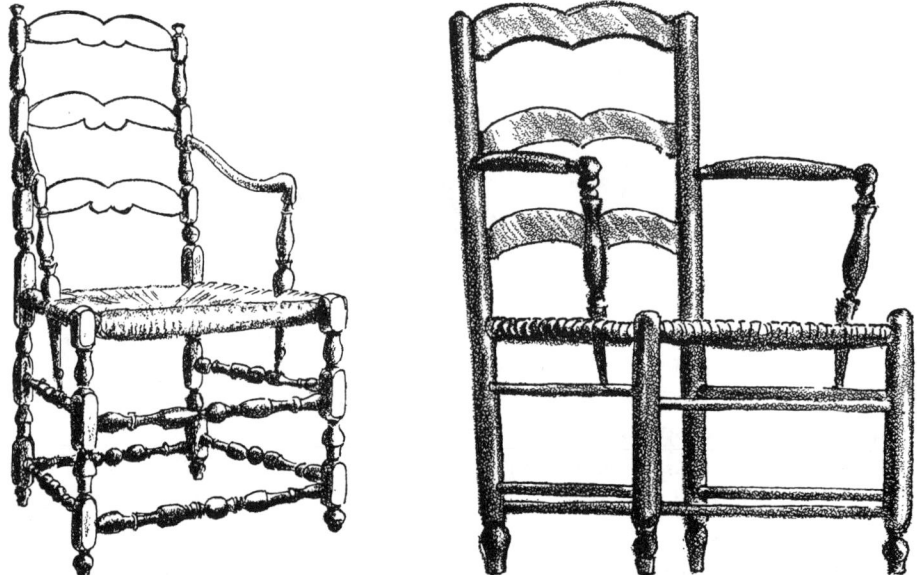

The salamander chair (left), considered by many the most beautiful slat-back chair ever designed, and a French Provincial rush-seated slat-back with separate arm supports, known as a two-bearing arm chair. Louis XV.

upholstered wing chair was introduced to the colonies. Some of the less finely constructed pieces were painted. Black was the favorite ground color, with designs in red, yellow, and white. Color was also introduced in the upholstery, the possible coverings consisting of leather, Turkey-work, velvet, tapestry, and for the first time, chintz (chints) was introduced. This was made by painting designs on linen or cotton cloth.

Black and gold were the elegant finishes, contrasting with delicate shades and tints of blue, yellow-green and rose red. The effect was quite as rich as the dull velvets and leathers of the earlier styles, but gayer and far less somber, and therefore more acceptable for modern use.

By the time the next English ruler, Queen Anne, came to the throne in 1702 the English craftsmen had absorbed and refined the William-and-Mary style till it was almost wholly English. During Queen Anne's 12-year reign this style was further refined so that it could at last justifiably take the name of Queen Anne itself. And in that form it arrived here. This period was the actual connecting link between the late 17th century and early 18th century styles, and became one of the most popular in the colonies at that time.

From what has been said thus far some idea can be gleaned of the basic

The primitive butterfly table, as popular today as in the 17th Century.

pieces of furniture available in the colonies before 1700. If you want your house to represent one of these early periods, these are the items you can use according to the degree of formality you wish to achieve. You will obviously have to add to those basic pieces many others that are similar in general style or otherwise compatible. That is a subject we can take up after we have briefly discussed the furnishing possibilities of succeeding periods, starting with the year 1700 A.D. which must be left to the next chapter.

5

THE SYBARITIC CENTURY: *The Queen Anne style—The Early Georgian era—Chippendale arrives—Hepplewhite to Sheraton—Duncan Phyfe—A Touch of French—American Bourgeois.*

The beginning of the 18th century found the better middle class houses for the first time furnished with some degree of comfort. The moderately well-to-do householder could then acquire all the William-and-Mary pieces hitherto unobtainable. Much more furniture was made in the colonies even though a great deal was still imported.

Within five years the more refined William-and-Mary style dubbed Queen Anne was coming to the fore. Among the most popular pieces were lowboys, highboys, slant-top desks, draw tables, tester beds, trundle beds, and a variety of chairs with comfortably shaped backs and soft seats of cane, reed, chip, leather, and needlework. For upholstered pieces damask and brocatelle were popular. Chintz and haircloth, and designs known as "furniture checks" were available in a variety of materials.

All this furniture was lighter and more delicate than the older pieces of oak. This was the Age of Walnut—though fruit and nut woods and maple were also used—of veneered woods, inlays, lacquering and japanning, bandy (cabriole) legs, and delicate carving.

Besides concentrating on walnut furniture construction, the makers during this period went all out for the cabriole leg which well suited the curved lines of the pieces. The Queen Anne chair had these legs at the front and curving square ones at the back. The seat was broad, and the back formed of a hairpin loop with a vase- or fiddle-shaped splat in the middle. This splat might be plain, pierced, or carved.

The whole high back was curved (spooned) to make it comfortable. The chair feet might be in the ball-and-claw, pad, scroll, or club style. On

Typical tilt-top table with pie-crust edge and claw feet.

chests the bracket foot was introduced, with swan-neck, scroll, or broken pediments, with or without a turned finial at the center.

Among the larger pieces that came into common use were ceiling-high secretaries, tallboys, and lowboys used for dressing tables. Some of these items were finished in Chinese lacquer and beautifully decorated. Some upholstered chairs were accompanied by a large "squab" cushion that to all intents turned them into a *chaise longue*.

Between 1702 and 1714, the Queen Anne Period, the style changed quite considerably. In the beginning the furniture was heavier, and pieces

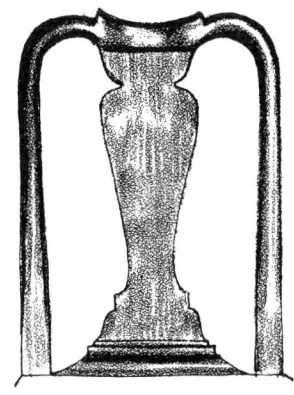

Vase-back of a Queen Anne style walnut chair dated about 1750.

with long legs, such as chairs and tallboys, had the legs strongly braced. In the middle years the designs were lighter and the bracing abolished. The pieces were plain and relied on delicacy of line and modeling for their beauty. Toward the end of the period, however, decoration was added. The knees of the legs were carved with cockle or scallop shell ornaments, and the early pad foot (the Dutch foot) was replaced by the claw-and-ball type.

The Early Georgian Era

From 1714 to 1749, a period which is called the Early Georgian era, the trend toward decoration increased. The simple Queen Anne pieces were now carved and fretted, gesso ornaments were applied. Some pieces were gilded, or painted in a variety of colors. Others were black japanned to imitate lacquer. Though velvet was always popular for chair upholstery, and red leather fast becoming popular among men, the late Queen Mary's hobby had started a vogue for needlepoint which had carried through Queen Anne's reign and lasted a long time after.

At this point in furniture history a notable event took place. While the designers and makers of fashionable furniture were busy with their traditional pieces, some Philadelphia chair makers interested in the general market, produced an improved version of the English Windsor chair. As a result of their efforts the Windsor was soon on its way to become the most popular chair in the country for general use. Intended for cottages it was at once in demand for country houses, and many modified designs were developed to extend its range of usefulness.

The seats of these Windsors were of thick pine or birch; the spindles and legs of maple, oak, beech, or ash. The bent parts may have been of ash, hickory, or birch. Some of the chairs were painted, others left in the raw wood or waxed, but whatever their finish a great many of them eventually found their way from the kitchen to the fashionable dining room. Today they are in greater demand than ever.

During the Queen Anne-Early Georgian Periods several furniture fashions changed. The vogue for tea drinking had created a demand for light portable tables, and so tea-tables came into being. The old desk boxes

Reproduction Chippendale side and arm chairs with the characteristic straight legs of the 1760–1775 period.

were replaced by secretaries of cherry, and later of mahogany; cupboards went out of style when high chests of drawers came in, and fancy looking glasses were popular as wall decorations with those who could afford them.

Furniture of this 1714–1749 period is of special interest to us today because so much of it is readily adaptable to modern homes and standards of living. In its various phases, the Queen Anne style can be applied to either informal or formal rooms with equal success. But this cannot be said of all the furniture developed during the Early Georgian phase.

By 1750 mahogany was fast growing to be the most popular cabinet wood, at least for the better class furniture. In England a designer destined to become the first cabinet maker after whom a furniture period was named, proclaimed it the king of cabinet woods. In all his work thereafter, Thomas Chippendale demonstrated the truth of that claim.

Chippendale Arrives

The growth to fame of the English wood carver, Thomas Chippendale, marked the end of the Early Georgian furniture styles both there and here. His furniture designs took both Britain and the colonies by storm. In 1754 he published his famous "Directory" and started a vogue that has persisted ever since.

Williamsburg reproduction of a Chippendale style wing chair in leather.

Graceful tea table of Queen Anne style with raised rim, scalloped edge, and slides for tea pots or urns.

A point that we so often overlook is that ninety per cent of the American furniture that we call Chippendale was made in this country by Colonial craftsmen for colonial homes. The same applies in a large degree to other furniture styles that were adopted here. But the furniture was good. It was made by craftsmen who had served their apprenticeships, whether in England, or the Continent, or here, under masters. Cabinet making was all they knew. Yet, of course, few of them were of the caliber of Chippendale, and other leading cabinetmakers of the time. They could copy, and to a small degree, improvise but they could not design. The exceptions were men like Goddard of Newport and Savery of Philadelphia. These master craftsmen took Chippendale's drawn designs and from them created and built pieces that Chippendale himself had never attempted to construct. The blockfront secretaries, chests, cabinets, and desks produced by Goddard, and Savery's elaborate highboys and lowboys have never been excelled.

Very few pieces of Chippendale's own work ever reached this country, and many of his published designs were never made by him. Nevertheless, ever since that day, any piece of furniture even remotely resembling a Chippendale design has been saddled with that name.

The Chippendale furniture developed into four distinct styles representing changes in the sources of his inspiration, successively from Queen Anne (English), to the French, Gothic, and Chinese. The English phase of Chippendale is the simplest and therefore the most adaptable to modern use in the average home. Chippendale chairs, which were wider, lower, and generally more comfortable than others of that day, were produced in astonishing variety. Some had straight legs, others, cabriole with the Georgian claw-and-ball, the lion's paw, or the turn-up French foot. Some had pierced splats, others the famous ribband backs, and so on. Chippendale's chairs undoubtedly were his best pieces, particularly in his earlier years before he began to over-embellish them.

The large number of so-called Chippendale pieces made in the American colonies during the last half of the 18th century included settees and sofas, some of them fully upholstered and with roll arms, others graceful and light in the French manner; imposing secretaries and breakfront bookcases; exquisite tilt-top tables with scalloped or piecrust edges.

Chippendale himself used the rich dark and very hard Honduras mahogany which lent itself admirably to his exquisite delicate carving. On the larger pieces he specified elaborately designed hardware, often of pierced brass. His cast brass finials gave that extra touch of elegance to his secretaries and mirrors that approached perfection. Apart from this he seems to have preferred to limit ornamentation to the carving he did so well.

In his Chinese phase Chippendale designed gilt and painted mirrors, hanging shelves in the bamboo and latticework motives, and straight-legged, fretwork-back chairs, covering both back and seat in tapestry. His later beds had exposed posts at the foot, and carved wood cornices, generally pierced.

Other pieces that he designed and which are popular in modern homes were mirrors, console tables, sandwich tables, corner cupboards, a settee with a back that looks like two chair backs joined together, and semi-upholstered arm chairs. Most of these pieces are obtainable in reproduction today.

Many of Chippendale's pieces are a little too elaborate for the modest home, but there are also a great many that are simple and well suited to the average dwelling of the Georgian style. Among the more readily recognized characteristics of his styles are the free use of carving, his fondness for and treatment of the cabriole leg with the ball-and-claw foot; the Chinese flavor of many of his pieces; the use of a straight square leg for some chairs, and the carved, often pierced, ladder and ribband backs which he also applied to beds and sofas.

Occasionally we hear references to a kind of furniture called Phila-

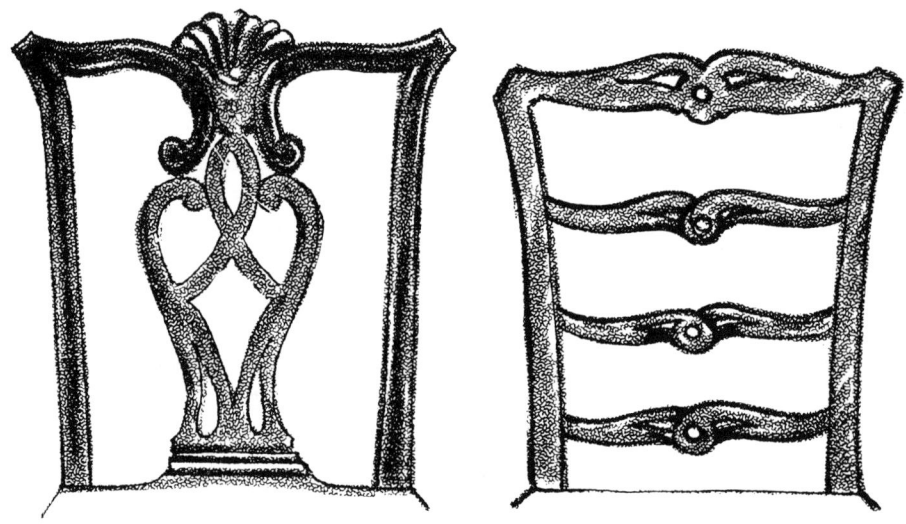

Characteristic Chippendale carved chair back design of the simpler type (left), and a Chippendale ladder-back.

delphia Chippendale. This originally was the product of a group of Philadelphia cabinet makers, most of whom came from England, in the last days of the Early Georgian era. These men made a variety of pieces in the Early Georgian manner, using the cabriole leg and ball-and-claw foot, and sometimes the French upturned roll foot. This Queen Anne furniture with a Georgian accent, was beautifully made in both walnut and mahogany, and found a ready market throughout Pennsylvania.

The original Philadelphia Chippendale, though basically Queen Anne, had a definite Chippendale flavor. This and many modified copies of Chippendale produced later may easily be mistaken for the true Chippendale by anyone but an expert. But unless you are an antique dealer it does not seem that this matters very much. True Chippendale and good copies or adaptations should look well together, and that is all that we can ask. The only requisite is that all the pieces be of first class workmanship and authentic in spirit, with finely executed detail. The one time it is important to know the special characteristics of any style is in buying reproductions of them.

Among the distinguished American cabinetmakers of the 18th century who added their individual touch to the basic English styles predominantly

Three commonly used decorative motives adopted by Hepplewhite: the Prince of Wales feathers, the swag, and bellflower husks. Sheraton used the oval, lyre and vase shapes, lattice, swag, conch shell and leaf patterns.

those of Chippendale, probably the best known are John Goddard of Newport, William Savery of Philadelphia, and Samuel McIntire of Salem.

There are many fine reproductions made of all the period furniture, but there are also plenty of cheap imitations that have none of the qualities that make the originals great. Detecting the difference is an art. It can also be lots of fun.

Hepplewhite to Sheraton

Chippendale himself was active till 1779. Meanwhile, in 1760, another great English furniture designer, George Hepplewhite, began to influence colonial furniture styles. But it was not till the end of the Revolutionary War that he came into his own on this side of the Atlantic.

By that time many Americans were tired of Chippendale's fretwork and Chinese pagodas, and many other reminders of Colonial days. The fresh, clean line of Hepplewhite's delicate pieces, decorated with inlays and painted panels, were a welcome change. For one thing, he catered to others besides the very rich, and a great many of his pieces were shipped to the new Republic where they were reproduced in astonishing quantities.

Hepplewhite went in for less elaborate detail and simpler forms than Chippendale. His carving was less complicated and he seemed to prefer decorative inlays and borders. In many pieces he substituted satinwood, or other exotic woods, for the commoner mahogany. In some of his designs the influence of the French styles of Louis XV and XVI is so evident that they are termed French Hepplewhite. In these pieces the cabriole legs are lighter, and the sweeping curves melt into the frame without a break.

On other pieces Hepplewhite used the turned and fluted legs characteristic of the Louis XVI style. One piece of furniture that he is supposed to have developed is the sideboard with cupboards and drawers. A characteristic detail is the shield-shaped back of his chairs and the motives he most commonly employed in his inlays and carvings were: The Prince of Wales feathers, wheat cluster, pendant husks, and swag garlands.

Other Hepplewhite features are straight, tapering legs, often fluted or reeded, with spade or thimble feet; serpentine curves in otherwise rectangular pieces such as furniture tops and cornices. His shield-back chairs with straight front legs and rearward sweeping back ones are typical examples of his designs. He made bow-fronted cabinets and serpentine sideboards with oval inlays for decoration.

The curved splay of the bracket feet he used on chests of drawers is a typical Hepplewhite detail. His sofas had outward curving ends in wood and six or eight legs with no suspicion of a stretcher to detract from their slender grace. He used mahogany, satinwood, and various veneers and inlays. Probably the best known of his pieces was the small drop-leaf table called a Pembroke, which he did much to popularize.

Though Hepplewhite produced some of the most beautifully proportioned furniture, much of it we should consider too delicate for everyday use in homes where sizeable or ungentle men would expect to relax. For formal settings it could not be improved upon.

Here we should perhaps, for the record, mention the Adam brothers, the architects who were Hepplewhite's principal influence. Chippendale had made furniture for Robert Adam who believed that an architect's true function was not only to design a house but also everything in it. Since he built only mansions and palaces, his extremely classic designs are of little interest to the small-house owner today. Occasionally we do find an Adam mantel or some other interior detail that can be attributed to him, but his furniture is of little interest here.

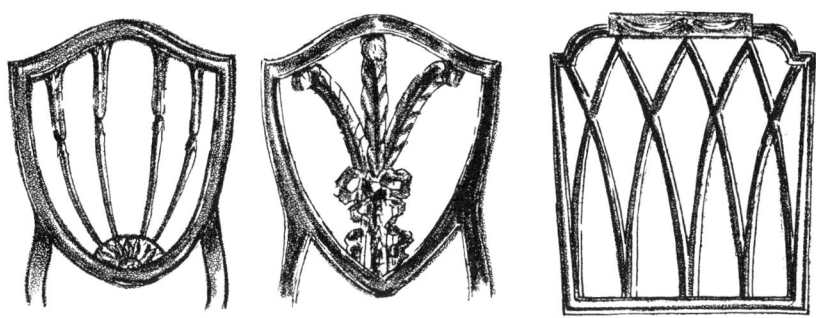

Typical Hepplewhite shield-backs (left), and a Sheraton cathedral-back adaptation of an Adam design.

About four years after Hepplewhite's death in 1786, the work of another top furniture maker began to attract attention in America. This was Thomas Sheraton, a man of many parts, as they used to say. He was for long an itinerant preacher, but he had a rare gift for design. He made some of the Adam ideas practical for others besides princes and the heirs of Croesus. In the beginning he actually made furniture himself, but later spent his time drawing designs for other cabinetmakers to use.

His pieces often were more delicate even than Hepplewhite's, but he made up for that by the use of underbracing and other structural devices. Sheraton combined features of Louis XV furniture with those of Adam and Hepplewhite, and the result was a classic style that was not excessively for-

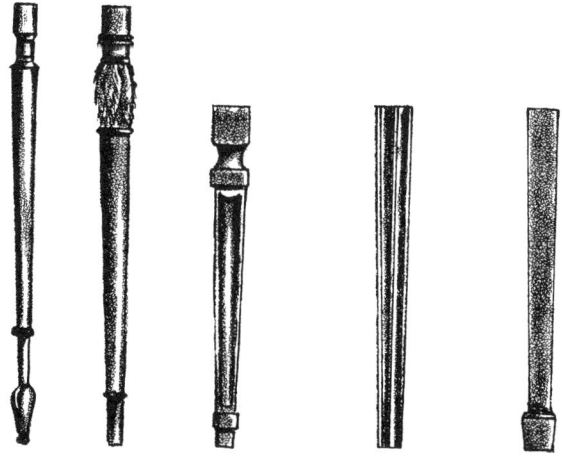

Three typical Hepplewhite (left) and two Sheraton type chair legs.

mal. His shield-back chairs differ in detail from those of Hepplewhite. Most of his chairs had square backs in which the bottom rail was raised well above the seat. The legs of the chairs were tapered, both in the round and square models, the round ones often being reeded. Either type might or might not have a spade foot. His table legs were sometimes made with a spiral turning.

Sheraton's specialty was what we might call boudoir furniture—kidney-shaped desks and tables; small chairs, some with oval backs and star-shaped splats, others having diamond, urn, or lyre pattern splats in a square frame. He designed many beds, including the forerunners of modern twin beds, called summer beds.

His later passion was for lacquered and painted furniture and straw-colored satinwood. In America birdseye and curly maple were used instead. Sheraton used very little carving, preferring porcelain plaques and borders of light wood, contrasting inlays and even inlaid brass.

Many of Sheraton's designs were used by furniture makers in America, and a large variety of chair designs is based on his drawings. Many of these chairs are suitable for the middle class home of today.

Hepplewhite and Sheraton styles are the two most likely to be confused and it is not easy to catalog their differences. Each of them produced pieces that favored the other's designs and treatment. Their main point of difference was that where Sheraton liked to use straight lines, Hepplewhite preferred curves. They both designed sideboards, and while Sheraton often curved his ends inward Hepplewhite reversed the curves, making them convex.

Many of the Hepplewhite pieces go very well with the Sheraton furniture and vice versa, so that errors in naming the style are of very little consequence.

Duncan Phyfe

The next designer to influence American furniture styles was Duncan Phyfe. Before coming to New York in 1790 he designed and built furniture in the style of Adam and Hepplewhite. He then turned to Sheraton and the French Directoire styles for his inspiration. From about 1800 to 1820 he built the furniture that made him famous and which is so much copied today. By 1820 the French Empire style, architectural and heavy, began to grow in popularity here. Phyfe developed his own interpretations of Empire, but even these were so lacking in grace that he was forced to admit that they deserved the epithet "butcher's furniture."

Sheraton design of drum table more common in England than in the Colonies. A piece for the more formal library or living room.

Sheraton style console or card table. The top swivels to open out flat.

Sheraton type end table. Note reeded front apron and inlaid drawer.

A late Sheraton style of sewing table offered in reproduction as a chair-side, occasional, or lamp table.

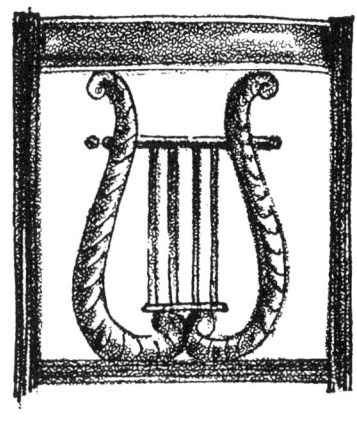

Sheraton chair back (left) of a late period, and the famed Phyfe lyre back, a motive also employed by Sheraton.

The best of Phyfe's work included many delightful chairs, tables and sofas. He used Grecian curves in the back and legs of chairs, and the lyre or eagle motives in the chair backs, in sofa arms, and in pedestals for small tables. Most of his table tops were curved. His principal wood was rich, red mahogany, often adorned with brass fittings, casters, etc. and the lyre strings were made of brass or whalebone.

After 1825 the Empire style suffered further from mechanization of industry. The furniture had to be modified in design to permit of production by machine, and individuality was lost. The metal decoration of French Empire was imitated in gold stencil work on painted backgrounds.

Between 1820 and 1850 an interesting and very useful chair for old-time rooms was made in Connecticut. This was a painted, stencil-decorated, pillow-back chair called the Hitchcock after its maker. Though definitely a 19th century product it is reminiscent of a Sheraton "fancy" chair and is quite at home among pieces of an earlier day.

A Touch of French

Mention of the French Empire style brings us to the consideration of another type of French furniture that was far more popular in parts of America from about 1710 to 1795. This early style is known as French Provincial, and has a distinct country flavor. In the early days, it was a favorite in French settlements such as Louisiana and parts of Delaware and Pennsylvania. Strangely enough the French Provincial style was based on the somewhat extravagant furniture styles rampant in France during the reigns of Louis XIV, XV, and XVI. Stripped of its ornate decoration, and produced in oak, ash, light walnut, pear, cherry, and apple wood, it lost almost all its sophistication. But the graceful outlines of the pieces remained.

The actual designs varied according to the *departement* or *province* from which the pieces came. And there were a tremendous number of them, from dough troughs to secretaries. The pieces suitable for small houses of today are of course quite limited in number. Since this style is popular with present day makers of reproductions you do not have to furnish wholly with antiques. Nor need you confine your furniture to French Provincial. Some of it suggests 17th century Cromwellian; other pieces favor Pennsylvania Dutch, and others the more delicate Queen Anne, with a touch here and there of Sheraton. It is these elusive suggestions of other styles—most of which have been influenced by the French at one time or another—that makes French Provincial so adaptable and such a good mixer.

American Bourgeois

Throughout the 18th century and well into the second quarter of the 19th there was a great deal of furniture produced that had little to do with the world's great designers or fashionable taste. This was the furniture of the common people throughout the colonies and later the country districts of 19th century America. This furniture was made by local carpenters, joiners, and even by untrained individuals for their own use. Itinerant joiners and chair makers travelled throughout the colonies making this furniture according to their own ideas, imitating formal designs that took their fancy, or copying existing pieces owned by their customers.

This unsophisticated country type of furniture is reproduced in large volume today and much used for summer homes and small country houses. A great deal of it is made of maple, some in cherry or pine, ash, or even whitewood. In the old days any available wood was used, such as ash, pine, maple, the fruit woods and nut woods.

The pieces most in demand evidently were chests of drawers, slant-top desks, slat-back chairs, flat-top highboys, lowboys, low-post beds, Sheraton type tables, adjustable candle stands, stools, hutch and chair tables, and so on. The origins of many of these pieces are quite unknown and it is fre-

Modern reproduction of a small Phyfe style drum table of mahogany with holly inlay.

quently impossible to date them with any degree of accuracy. Surviving
pieces of old-time workmanship however have long been in demand both by
collectors and those who need substantial antique pieces to give their country houses and town house kitchens a cheerful old-time flavor.

Of recent years there has also been a growing interest in other local
styles of furniture indigenous to America. Isolated settlements, and religious
groups in particular, contributed much that is worthwhile. One of the love-
liest styles of furniture ever made in this country was that of the sect called
the Shakers. Here severity in design has revealed the stark beauty of simplicity in its highest and most appealing form. The furniture is functional to
the utmost degree yet exquisite in line and proportion. Forms, tables, chairs,
reading desks, and simple four-square chests demonstrate the fascination of
perfect proportion and inspired symmetry unmarred by the slightest attempt
at decoration. This is something that very few of our modernist designers
have yet been able to achieve.

Far different in style and appeal is furniture of the Pennsylvania Dutch
origin which derives from early European forms. Sometimes finished plain
pine or walnut, much of this furniture is painted and decorated in colors with
devices that are pleasant and sentimental. Chests, corner, wall and spice cupboards, tables, chairs, benches, dough troughs, wall and pipe boxes, and so
forth, are standard items.

And so with the industrial revolution, America drifted into the Victorian age whose furniture we are only now beginning correctly to appraise.
Much of it was ugly and uninspiring, much more is lacking in comfort—
and pretentious. Yet there are certain pieces that can be used in "gingerbread
period" houses of the mid-century. The Victorian home, however, was much
overdressed, stuffy, and often downright ugly. If we are to furnish such a
house today we have to be extremely selective. We may even need to change
the appearance of some of the furniture by bleaching, painting, decorating,
adding colorful upholstery, and so on.

The Victorian house we can sometimes rescue from self-conscious ugli-
ness or garish frightfulness. We can tone down the flamboyant exterior
with a coat of white paint, but interiors usually call for drastic alterations.
Otherwise there is little worth the trouble in the average Victorian home.
The furniture of this era included most modern pieces plus a few that are
deservedly outmoded such as washstands with basin holes in the top, brass
beds decorated with mother-of-pearl, scrollwork whatnots, some very ugly
bronze and crystal girandoles, etc. *ad nauseam*. Some charming small settees

An attractive mid-18th Century Williamsburg grouping, suitable for the small hall or alcove.

and upholstered chairs reminiscent of the French Louis XV still deserve to be salvaged from this dusty era of glass beads, bamboo, and plush.

With other pieces, where the basic design is good, it may be possible to retrieve their usefulness by remodeling, removing some of the decoration, or perhaps bleaching the dark woods. Such odd pieces can then often be worked into an Early American or French Provincial setting.

6

STYLE SELECTION: *Choosing furniture to live with—Problems of suitability—Elizabethan days—James II or Jacobean—Primitive pieces—French Provincial—Dutch—English.*

Choosing the kind of furniture you are going to live with for years to come is almost like marrying or adopting a child. For most of us it represents a major milestone in our lives and constitutes a practically irrevocable step and an expensive one to boot!

From the moment you set the furniture into place your house has become a home, and the furniture the keynote to which you attune your scale of daily living. Your home, then, being the background against which your activities are projected, its furnishing demands a great deal of study and sober thought. The decision should not reflect a momentary mood, or vague nostalgic recollections of another home you once saw or lived in and enjoyed. You need a far more practical guide than that, and rules based on the experience of others who have made a study of such things can be of great help. But the final decisions, of course, will be yours. Houses that are homes cannot be furnished by rule of thumb. It is useful to remember this in view of what follows here.

If we have seemed to labor the point of matching the furniture to the house it is because so many handicap themselves by cheerfully ignoring that rule. Obviously, not all of the Colonial styles will suit every kind of house. There are those that cannot even be mixed without producing an undesirable effect. Some are more formal in design than others and call for backgrounds and accessories in keeping with their elegance. Still others are of classical feeling and decoration and therefore suited only to classical architecture and interiors. But among them all there is still a wide choice of furniture styles that can be used with informal interiors and small rooms.

Dangerous as it is to generalize, we may perhaps hazard a few opinions which, however, may need modifying to meet any particular case. One of the more obvious of these is that Pilgrim furniture does not look well in a stately Georgian setting (though we have seen it tried), nor do the rich mahogany pieces of Revolutionary days seem happy alongside the batten doors and rough plaster of a New England farm house. This principle can be extended considerably further. For instance, in houses of the northern Early American type, the informal furniture of any period from 1650 to 1800 may satisfactorily be utilized. This may be Early Colonial, Jacobean, early Queen Anne, or American Provincial of any period including Pennsylvania Dutch and Shaker. Any of the old-time plain furniture of common American woods, or perhaps informally painted, will look well. Pieces made of mahogany or inlay will not.

In the more formal Southern Early American and the Georgian types of houses, Elizabethan and William-and-Mary pieces may be used if the house is large; Jacobean if it is not. The later decorated Queen Anne, or mahogany furniture of any subsequent style will be eminently suitable.

For the American houses of Greek Revival architecture, less ornate and classically more severe furniture is called for, such as the late Hepplewhite and Sheraton that show the Adam influence, the French Empire, or Duncan Phyfe's interpretations of the French Directoire.

These are broad generalizations. It is only when you get down to specific instances that difficulties arise. There are exceptions and important ones, and these can only properly be illustrated by examples, such as we shall introduce later. But first there is the question of approach.

You may be one of the lucky few who are able to face the subject of furnishing your Old American house with an open mind, free of style preferences and prejudices, or you may have a strong predilection toward some particular style or period. In either case when you come to study the subject you soon find that there are several things to be considered that were not at first apparent and which may well change your whole idea. One of the most immediate of these is just how far you will have to deviate from the style or period that you incline to in order to get a fully and comfortably furnished home.

If, for example, you are thinking of going back to the very beginning of things, to the earliest Colonial days of New England, you will not, of course, be able to furnish your house completely in Pilgrim style. And you would not be very comfortable if you did! Then, again, it may be that you have decided that since your rooms are small you cannot hope to use furniture of any but the most informal kind such as the later American Provincial. But a little consideration will show that not all small rooms are or need to be ultra-informal; size is never the whole criterion.

Room size does, of course, set certain limits on what you can and cannot do. Some styles such as William-and-Mary are by nature expansive, and they lose a great deal when they are reproduced in sizes smaller than the originals. Therefore this style of furniture is not suited to small rooms, particularly if the ceilings are not high.

But, like most rules for furnishing, even that one is subject to exceptions. It is quite possible to use one or two William-and-Mary pieces in a small room—and by small we mean not less than 15 feet square—rounding out with pieces of another but sympathetic syle. For example, you might have a William-and-Mary chest, or cabinet that you would not want to part with and must find a place for. That could very well be the dominant piece in a man's den or study, maybe balanced by a built-in bookcase. The rest of the furniture could include a Queen Anne wing chair, or a Pilgrim wainscot chair or tall slat-back chair. Even sturdy hoop-backed Windsors would not look amiss!

Jacobean furniture with the turned instead of spiral legs, especially in the lighter oak finish, would be an excellent foil, particularly in a gateleg table or similar piece. Even the more modern upholstered chairs and sofas would not seem out of place with the cabinet or chest.

Your main problem in such a room would of course be to avoid an over-furnished look. If you use large pieces you need to have fewer of them; and a nice balance as to height and placing of them.

To go to the other extreme, a large room furnished with many small pieces looks cluttered, and the furniture pieces themselves become insignificant. Such a room then looks more like a furniture store than part of a home.

A room that is properly furnished contains all that is necessary for use and comfort and yet it leaves breathing space for its occupants. This means that the furniture you use should be of sizes and proportions compatible with the floor space and wall height. Scale, then, is important and must be taken into account in deciding on your furniture style. This is not to say that a great deal cannot be done to make small rooms *look* larger, or larger ones appear small. It *can*, and we shall go into details on that later. Right now the subject is factors affecting the choice of style.

Next in importance after scale comes the degree of formality you would like the room to express. Here is where you consider each room

Early Colonial entry featuring a Connecticut chest and 17th Century leather-covered chairs, probably of European origin.

separately. Few houses are uniformly furnished throughout. The parlor is likely to be a little stiffer than the keeping room, and the kitchen less formal than either, while a study may well be given over to solid comfort or, at the other extreme, pure practicality. In the bedrooms you can have stark masculinity or frilly femininity, cozy intimacy or cool dignity, or any shade of feeling in between.

But, regardless of all this, in the smaller houses there needs to be a certain amount of unity of furniture style. You don't want Elizabethan oak in the master's den and Hepplewhite inlaid mahogany in the dining room; the contrast is too extreme. On the other hand, you can equip each room with furniture of a different style or period providing there is some obvious relationship between the kinds of furniture such as general lines, color, or surface texture.

Both the degree of formality and the general mood of a room can be influenced tremendously by the background and accessories. Therefore in furnishing the small house, where some definite and obvious relationship between the rooms is essential, the same or similar furniture often can be used throughout. What differences there must be can be contrived by added materials and colors, decorative features and ornaments.

This concentration on one period as the main theme of the furnishing will then give the whole house the desired old-time atmosphere augmented by the charm of mellow antiquity.

No doubt many personal reasons will enter into your final choice of a furniture style, but if your choice is to give you lasting satisfaction your furniture will have to bear a close relation to your style of living and your circumstances as well as to your house. Fine furniture needs care and attention, but what is equally important it needs living up to. The furnishings must match the quality and the style of furniture, and a formal furniture demands a dignified style of living.

If you are the outdoors type of family, or have a troop of healthy, boisterous children, you are most likely to want furniture that needs a minimum of attention and can stand rough usage. It must be sturdy in design and have a finish that is not easily marred. Nothing looks worse than fine furniture badly used and out of key with the household it serves. For such a home your choice will doubtless be for rugged pieces of informal or even primitive style. But if you are socially inclined, in a mature fashion, and given to formal or semi-formal entertainment, you may want furniture that speaks of a sophisticated taste and exudes an air of luxury.

Luckily there are Colonial styles that meet the demands of these two extremes and almost any furnishing requirement between them, given the requisite accessories and background without which no furnishing scheme can be successful or complete.

With these considerations in mind, then, perhaps we can look into some possible combinations of interiors and furniture that will meet these varying needs.

Elizabethan Days

The earliest American Colonial houses were put up by men to whom the massive furniture of the days of Good Queen Bess was the most familiar. The houses were small by modern standards even in the Virginia colony. But they were sturdy, and the wood interiors formed a fitting background for the heavy, rectangular, lavishly carved pieces. With the rich, dark materials used for hangings and for draping over chests, for the chair and back cushions, the total effect was one of somber magnificence. In the smaller houses it must have been overpowering, and that no doubt is why folding and collapsible pieces were so much in demand.

In houses with higher ceilings and whitewashed walls above a paneled wainscot the individual pieces of furniture showed to best advantage. The continuous horizontal line of the wainscot tied the room together, and heavy tapestry hangings balanced the taller pieces. The total effect was splendid and even the smaller rooms had an air of magnificence that we should find rather appalling today.

For essentially American houses, even those that cling to the English flavor, the Elizabethan is, in this day and age, a little too overpoweringly medieval. What we can do, however, is to use odd pieces that are not too massive, and perhaps combine them with the lighter, early Jacobean specimens that have the same feeling on a smaller and less pretentious scale.

There are available today some excellent reproductions of Elizabethan (or Tudor) refectory tables that look well in a home library or behind a heavy sofa, or used in place of a sideboard along a wall. Some other Elizabethan pieces that might be used are the smaller carved chests, high-backed chairs, and benches.

Today most of us like more air and light in our rooms than our ancestors were content with, and large pieces of furniture cast too many deep shadows on the floor. Therefore if we admire the spirit of Elizabethan furniture we use it to furnish only the very largest of rooms, or use a piece here and there—in an entrance hall, for example—or else substitute the less ponderous Jacobean.

James II or Jacobean

Since some few pieces of Jacobean furniture were brought into New England, and a great deal of it imported into Virginia, it is a permissible style for some early Colonial houses. After a while, however, the early Colonial carpenters began to get ambitious. They broke away from Puritan tradition and went in for furniture decoration in a large way. It is perhaps a coincidence that their later decorated chests, for example, looked very much like some of the English Jacobean ones.

The Colonials applied split spindles to the chest panels, as in the case of the Hadley chest, and the English craftsmen used applied moldings, but the general effect is the same. Other Jacobean chests were both decorated with moldings and carved all over as some Colonial chests were. Other Colonial pieces with a Jacobean air were the joint stools and small tables. The stools nowadays are used as low occasional or coffee tables as well as seats. Both Jacobean and the early colonial craftsmen produced gateleg tables, and the Colonial butterfly table was a variation that takes its name from the shape of its drop-leaf support.

These similarities between the Jacobean originals and primitive Colonial copies of them suggest two things. One is that the Jacobean can very well be used in Colonial rooms, and the other is that they may be mixed, providing a proper selection is made. The Jacobean, naturally, is more sophisticated in manner and more formal in feel. To do either of them justice the background and accessories must be in keeping. Beams, wood floors, and paneling constitute the normal setting for both.

Strangely enough, some Jacobean pieces lend themselves equally well to formal or informal rooms. Jacobean tables with twisted legs will look well almost anywhere—in a mansion or a country cottage—providing the setting is right. The Jacobean style, incidentally, provides sufficient pieces to permit the complete furnishing of a house. The Early Colonial, unfortunately, does not.

Primitive Pieces

The furniture that we call primitive is the not-always naked (some was painted) but generally unadorned product of artisans from the Pilgrim era to the early 19th century.

In the early days a great many single pieces of unique design were made, but the element of simplicity, the woods used, and certain details of construction common to many of them enable us to assemble a variety of pieces that go well together in Early Colonial rooms. These pieces are exclusively for the informal house.

Into the collection we can garner the earliest wainscot chair, and spindle chairs of the Brewster, Carver, and turned-spindle-back types, plus early ladder backs. The scratch-carved or painted chests can be put in the hall or at the foot of a bed (where they can be used without having things put on the lid); and we can use in several rooms the simple turned-leg joint stools, candle stands and small tables; open and closed shelf cupboards, paneled oak bedsteads, oak tavern tables, and so forth.

If you want sofas to go with this very early furniture you are practically forced to use spindle-back settees, that look like two or three chairs joined together, or a later spindle-back settle. Alternatively you can adapt a pine fireside settle, properly cushioned, or a day bed of the simplified Jacobean type, or one that favors the folding press bed. But these two latter would have no back and would need to be used against a wall and not in front of a fireplace.

Any of these pieces that you can use together should be either all of oak, or all pine or ash, but you can mix them if the woods are of the same general tone. Even more important than the color is the similarity in "feel" between the pieces. The old oak pieces usually were thicker and heavier than similar pieces in lighter weight woods, in keeping with the traditional sturdiness of the oak tree.

You can also use waxed ash, birch, or even some kinds of unfinished maple that time has given a yellowish brown patina that does not jar with the oak. We say plain maple because hard maple does not take well to waxing or oiling.

When you get into the later primitive furniture you can use a great many pieces that are less primitive in feel and more strictly provincial. One perennial favorite for rooms later than 1725 is the Windsor chair. It goes well with almost anything, but particularly with turned gateleg tables. For earlier rooms you would have to use a simple banister-back style of chair or the very earliest slat-backs.

In addition to the early tavern tables with turned legs and various kinds of stretchers, there are also a great many hutch tables, chair tables, and small tables on turned pedestals with legs of various types. Candle stands, useful for other things as well, were likewise an early piece, as were plain pine slant-top desks and tall-post beds with or without canopies.

All of this furniture obviously demands the simplest unaffected background—plenty of rough white plaster and oak and pine, and simple trim

Antique dining room with an atmosphere of great charm. Early and late 18th Century furniture is combined with pieces of the early 1800s. Wall accessories contribute to the general air of authenticity.

with early hardware. Much of the same thing applies to the later maple furniture, but the period will be more modern, calling for plastered walls without so much woodwork in evidence, painted trim and plastered ceilings. Here you can have dressers in maple, pine or cherry, arrowback chairs, turned spindle chairs, arm chairs with tied-on cushions for back and seat, chests of drawers, low-post beds and field beds.

Then you get into the early 19th century, a period that furniture manufacturers have combed for examples of primitive pieces to reproduce in birch and maple. Such pieces are comparatively cheap to produce, and the result has been the flooding of the market with rubbish. Nevertheless you can get excellent reproductions of this Early American furniture if you know what you are looking for. Cheap and gaudy finishes are to be avoided, as are the spectacular pieces with over-fancy turnings and other exaggerated features.

Included among this modern furniture are many pieces that our fore-fathers never dreamed of, and if you want to recapture the old-time flavor it is better to avoid them. Platform rockers, upholstered rockers, semi-upholstered settees, and arm chairs with wooden wings are among the worst offenders. The greatest drawback to most of these "reproductions" and adaptations is the fact that they do not look ancient enough to be authentic. They are old-fashioned but obviously not old, and their pristine air gives a room the appearance of forced naiveté and self-conscious posturing.

Only one or two makers, so far as we know, come anywhere near to reproducing the antique finish without which no reproduction is convincing. Of course if you are not attempting to recapture an old-time air or fit your furniture to an old house, this does not matter at all. Fortunately, with the more expensive mahogany and walnut reproductions the makers have more latitude in this respect. Whether or not they take advantage of it is something else again. There are poor expensive reproductions as well as good ones in all styles of furniture.

Any Colonial or Early American room of charm and authenticity should certainly look as though it had been in existence at least a hundred years. If the Early American reproductions do not have that appearance, or if they look cheap and poorly designed you are better off with some well-made modern design of American informal furniture, or even old French Provincial. The backgrounds can be the same though the accessories may differ.

French Provincial

The term French Provincial covers a wide variety of furniture designs just as American Provincial does. But the pieces we are interested in are the 18th century provincial interpretations of the French Louis XV style. They follow closely the lines of the furniture made for the aristocrats of that period, minus the decoration and applied ornament. Some of the pieces naturally have been simplified and in other ways adapted; nevertheless in very many pieces the excellence of the original design is not wholly lost.

The chairs in particular vary considerably in detail, and some of them combine readily with Queen Anne furniture while others are more at home with Pilgrim or Early American pieces. Some of the earlier side and arm chairs for example have turned legs and stretchers, turned side posts, and slat backs and rush seats. The more elegant ones betray their Louiv XV origin in the curved legs and shaped backs, but very often they too have rush seats. Those that were subject to the Louis XVI influence however may have tapered and fluted legs. Others are a peculiar combination of formal and informal, having plain turned legs and spindle stretchers, with a lyre back and straw seat! There is also a wooden settee that looks like three chairs with separate backs and bowed fronts. This has turned legs and curved arms, and though the seats are straw they are hidden beneath loose cushions, and each back is padded.

There are of course many upholstered pieces in this series, gay with check plaids, crewel work, or printed cotton—all of obvious peasant origin. The old-time colors are used in all their strength—crimson, green, and jonquil yellow! The furniture woods are mostly light in tone—apple wood, pear wood, and nut woods, including walnut, and also oak.

The more important pieces of furniture have a certain grace due to the sweeping curves of outlines and molding. Even the panels are curved into irregular shapes; and the hardware carries out the same feeling. On oak pieces the handles and hinges may be of brass but on the fruitwoods they are likely to be of polished steel. And finally, the typical French Provincial accessories such as knife boxes, bread boxes, and wall shelves have great decorative value in any simple room.

This type of furniture was used not only in the former French possessions in what is now the United States, but also in French Canada. It is perhaps the only definitely foreign style except the Pennsylvania Dutch that looks perfectly at home in a simple old Colonial house.

Dutch English

Solid comfort with a masculine air was the major characteristic of William-and-Mary furniture. The rich walnut looked best against white plaster walls and white painted woodwork and paneling, tile-surrounded fireplaces, and bare floors. Such a room would need rich hangings, and perhaps the dark canvases of old portraits.

A fair-sized dining room furnished in William-and-Mary style would not need many imposing pieces. Perhaps a flat-topped highboy with trumpet-turned legs and curved stretchers; turned chairs with square padded seats and backs, with carved crestings and rush seats; a lowboy used as a sideboard, and perhaps a tall clock to balance the highboy.

There would naturally be a good deal of formality in such a room, and to reduce that you would have to tone down the background. Less paneling, more bare plaster, and naked brick around the fireplace would make a start. Darker woodwork and trim would subdue the heavy pieces so that they did not stand out so boldly, and perhaps counteract the effect of a low ceiling that a simple house most likely would have.

But the best solution of all, in our experience, is to mix in a little Queen Anne. Smaller scale furniture with less rigid lines and greater variety would soften the whole room and supply an air of intimate charm that, with the undiluted William-and-Mary, can rarely be achieved.

And so, with Queen Anne, we enter on the 18th century and the beginning of the Georgian era, a project that calls for a separate chapter to itself.

7

STYLES AND INTERIORS: *Queen Anne to Phyfe—1712–1749*
—1749–1779—1779–1806—Composite rooms.

Selecting a furniture style from those dated after 1700 is somewhat simpler than trying to recreate a 17th century home. For one thing the later styles are more adaptable to modern living; they also provide a more complete range of pieces and fit into a variety of backgrounds.

The first of the 18th century styles, that named after Queen Anne, brings with it lighter and more cheerful colors. These are, for the most part, bright primary colors which we do not seem to use enough of nowadays. At any rate they set off the walnut furniture to advantage and give life to plain rooms of the period.

A large number of upholstered pieces is available for use and various degrees of formality are secured through the materials with which they are covered. Damasks, brocades, chintzes, and plain linens were the vogue, plus the earlier fabrics such as velvet, petit point needlework, cane and rush seating. Comfort is emphasized in the spring seats and soft cushions and, for the first time, modern upholstered pieces begin to look at home among the old-time furniture.

Lowboys matching the tallboys in the dining room find new uses as hall tables, dressing tables, etc. The tables, china cupboards, upholstered stools, benches and sofas make dining and living rooms really livable in the 20th century sense.

All of this Queen Anne furniture has a certain amount of dignity inherent in its beauty of line and the softness of its gentle curves. Therefore it is by nature neither grandly formal nor primitively informal. Rooms furnished with it have a certain manner, and it is necessary to rely on the upholstery and background fabrics, as well as the architectural features and textures of the room surfaces to influence it in either direction.

If you want an informal room with Queen Anne furniture you can use the linens and chintzes. If you prefer more formality you can employ the richer fabrics. The furniture will do them both justice. In the later Queen Anne days you can also choose between white plaster and paint and the early wall and paint colors. As a rule we prefer white plaster and a little natural woodwork in the small house.

In that setting, the waxed walnut, and the crown glass (if you can get it) of the closed cabinets have a certain glow in the daytime and a fascinating gleam in the flicker of fire- and candle-light.

In the later Queen Anne of the Early Georgian era, with its painted, decorated and marquetry pieces, some of this charm is lost, and a feeling of simplicity is not so easily obtained. However, since this later furniture has suffered from the classic French influence it is quite in order to lump it with the Early Georgian style into which it was gradually transformed. Actually it is part of a new and somewhat jumbled style.

1712–1749

The furniture of the transition period from Queen Anne to early Chippendale, which we call Early Georgian, included many experiments in furniture design. But there were lots of interesting pieces produced both in walnut and mahogany that could be included in a Queen Anne room or even in a Chippendale room.

The "Philadelphia Chippendale," and even the "Irish Chippendale" go with the later pieces to which the master's name is more justifiably attached. But the carving, fretting, gilding, and painting in red, blue, and green; the black japanning to imitate Chinese lacquer, are not finishes that seem adapted to the simple American home.

On the other hand, when we are dealing with the ornamented cabriole-legged chairs of the pre-Chippendale era, and similar pieces, we may as well include them with Chippendale's own work and the rest of the orphan pieces with which his reputation is commonly saddled.

1749–1779

Furnishing with Chippendale is an old story in American homes, even though very few actual Chippendale pieces were ever imported. The stores are full of Chippendale style furniture—and a great deal of mahogany junk that the master would have repudiated with horror. But mahogany is a fascinating wood, irresistible to those unsophisticated home-makers to whom it represents the epitome of elegance. And these are fair game for unscrupu-

Authentic reproduction of a chest-on-chest with the Hepplewhite touch.

lous manufacturers who can hide shoddy workmanship and design under a superabundance of machine carving. The first requisite, therefore, in furnishing a Colonial house with modern Chippendale, or alleged Colonial pieces of the Chippendale school, is to make sure of the quality of the furniture.

And there is an easily detectible difference between a machine produced piece and one that is finished by hand. All that you need to do is to examine a few good authentic pieces in museums or private collections, and note the details of carving, its sharpness, the fitting together of the pieces, and the color of the wood and its patina. On the piece you contemplate buying look for slopped red stain on the under parts, and avoid the deep red, highly-glossed finishes. Good reproductions are much browner and the gloss is satiny soft and seems in the wood rather than on top of it. The red mahogany you can leave to Phyfe.

The effects achieved by furnishing with Chippendale pieces are largely controlled by selection. You can get very early Chippendale in walnut, or later, in mahogany. You may have the simple pieces or the more lavishly decorated ones, and choose between the English, Gothic, French, and Chinese periods. By careful choice of harmonious pieces you may also mix them to a reasonable degree.

The later Queen Anne, some of the early Georgian, and practically all of the Chippendale pieces have enough elegance to look well in the formality of a Georgian architectural setting. Such settings are usually characterized by stately rooms with complicated moldings, decorated trim, higher ceilings of decorated plaster, taller windows, paneled wainscots, formal mantels, massive paneled and pedimented doors, built-in corner or wall cupboards, and so on. Alternatively you might have all walls paneled, with dentiled cornices. Such interiors would very well suit the most elaborate of the Chippendale and crypto-Chippendale pieces.

Contrary to what one would expect from all this, the more typical Chippendale pieces are robust enough to make themselves at home in humble surroundings. But rough floors need to be hidden and other crudities suppressed.

With the Chinese Chippendale our fancy is for less woodwork on the walls, and the ceiling-to-floor plaster covered with architectural paper, with or without a paper dado. The paper would have a Chinese touch such as a bamboo diaper or delicate pagoda pattern. There are a number of old ones of this type available.

In the smaller houses, and particularly the central-chimney type, the

Chippendale furniture needs handling with care. It will never look wholly at home for the clean simplicity of Early Colonial is so far removed from the colorful Oriental. But it can be done if due attention is paid to color, and the little formal touches introduced wherever possible. Fabrics and floor coverings of course play a decisive part. It is perhaps ironic that we should have to go back to the early 1700s for the use of primitive red paint for the interior. Few modern paints give so well the effect that ties in the early woodwork with the flavor of Old Cathay.

There is, of course, plenty of precedent for Chinese interiors since the days when Canton was a scheduled port of call for our sailing ships. Indeed, Chinese porcelains and fabrics and oriental rugs transformed many a New England home and Southern mansion. But today we need a better excuse for introducing exotic styles into old American homes.

1779–1806

As the 18th century wears out it becomes more and more difficult to adapt furniture fashions to the small house. But by the time of the Revolution, most of such houses did have a little more formality in their interiors. The windows had larger panes and the rooms more light. Bare beams were largely gone and posts hidden in walls; plaster was smoother and the best rooms had more decorative baseboards and perhaps panels under the windows. Gaping bake ovens had doors, and fireplaces were less cavernous. Wall decoration with stencils, paint, and even paper was both practical and common, and new floor finishes and covering materials were constantly being introduced. Altogether the home-maker had a much wider scope for prettying-up the house than even her mother had.

The furniture designer, however, did not cooperate so well as he might have done. A classic feeling in the air produced the antithesis of farmhouse styles. Fortunately, by this time, there also existed or were well on their way, the provincial pieces that we can turn to when Hepplewhite, Sheraton, and Phyfe fail to meet our demands.

However we regard them, it cannot be denied that the products of Hepplewhite and Sheraton at least are difficult to reconcile with the old-time Colonial interiors. In this respect such of the old houses as have been remodeled or restored, or the modern reproductions of Colonial houses, have a distinct advantage. The interior finish is smooth and fresh looking, and therefore more formal than those built and assembled long ago.

The houses built within a decade of 1800 are likely to have larger and better proportioned rooms and higher ceilings than the earlier ones. The

Reproduction Sheraton pembroke table with convenient drawer and side extensions, a style much favored as a sofa end-table.

Georgian interiors were architecturally more classical and less romantic (but doubtless more romanesque, thanks to Mr. Jefferson!), and therefore more suited to these furniture styles than those built earlier. But the Graeco-Roman influence evident in the later Hepplewhite and most of Sheraton's pieces makes them even more at home in a Greek Revival atmosphere. For a Greek Revival style of house these two furniture styles, either singly or intelligently mixed, are ideal.

And so if you have a Greek Revival or Georgian house with these advantages you probably can adopt Hepplewhite and Sheraton styles with just as much success as with the less delicate Phyfe. But you will need to see that the background details are as refined as the furniture designs, and suit your room colors to the upholstery materials.

The classical air of the early Phyfe furniture puts it largely into the same category as Hepplewhite and Sheraton, but there is some difference. For one thing its comparative sturdiness makes it acceptable in homes where the other two types would be considered too formal, too delicate, and perhaps too effeminate.

Strangely enough Phyfe furniture can look well in both a Georgian and a Greek Revival setting, and some pieces are eminently suitable for earlier and smaller houses. This apparent universality accounts to a large degree for Phyfe's popularity, but you need to be certain that you have authentic reproductions that are well made. For some people the Phyfe style loses much of its appeal simply because it is met with everywhere. But this is not so important if you know how to get individuality into your rooms, and to submerge the style in an interesting general effect.

Composite Rooms

In very few small houses is it possible to restrict the furniture to one style. Even if you have no heirlooms that simply must be accommodated somewhere, you are almost certain to need the additional cosiness and comfort that a modern piece of upholstered furniture affords. In acquiring such a piece—a process that should be left till the style of the rest of the furniture is decided upon—it is best to choose something that has the general lines and feel of the other pieces. That is to say, you should not expect a delicate Sheraton pembroke to look happy alongside a bulging overstuffed sofa, or an Early American ladder-back to set off the charms of a low-backed arm chair upholstered in mohair or rep.

The modern furniture, if it *must* be used, should be covered in old style materials of the colors and textures of the antique or reproduction pieces. Its exposed wood, such as legs, back rail, etc., should be finished to match the wood of the old furniture.

When it comes to mixing different styles of old furniture it is hardly possible to generalize on the results you may expect. So much depends upon the woods used and the main characteristics of the pieces concerned. Normally, however, it would be expected that pieces of the following styles would not be too antagonistic, viz:

> William-and-Mary and Queen Anne
> William-and-Mary and Jacobean
> Late Queen Anne and Chippendale
> Jacobean and Pilgrim
> Hepplewhite and Sheraton
> Phyfe and Chippendale

But you have to use considerable judgment even with these combinations. Not every piece has the desired features that characterize the style or period to which it belongs. If the woods are the same, or similar in color and texture, it is a big advantage, but there should be some closer relationship even than that. Ordinarily, old maple and cherry and pine can be used side by side, but in present-day furniture the differences may be painfully obvious because of the strange and wonderful finishes sometimes applied to them. The only sure guide then is a direct comparison of the pieces you want to use together.

8

THE SETTING: *The early use of paints and colors—17th and 18th century fabrics—Wall decoration—Stencilled walls—The first wallpapers—Choosing the paper—Floor treatment—Colored floors—Floor coverings.*

In the previous two chapters we have discussed the relation of the furniture to the bare interior of a room. But, as we are all well aware, we do not in this civilized age, content ourselves with disposing furniture in an empty shell. On the contrary, we go to great lengths to make the entire inside of a room an integral part of its furnishing.

We have spoken of plaster walls, wood walls and panels, and also of painted wood surfaces; of beamed, paneled or plastered ceilings; and of pine and oak floors. But even in copying the most primitive interior we find it necessary to do something about these expansive areas. The wooden floors we oil, or wax, or paint, or cover with carpeting, rugs, linoleum, or some other semi-permanent substance. The walls we whitewash, paint in white or color, or hide beneath wallpaper. Ceiling plaster likewise we can whiten, or paint or paper; and beams can be stained and antiqued or painted. At the windows we hang various decorative materials ostensibly to keep out drafts or light or both.

In all of these things the purpose is or should be to imitate the old-time finishes and decorations, or at least to recapture through suggestion the atmosphere those finishes and decorations helped give to the room. At the same time we seek to provide an authentic setting for the furniture of the period we choose.

The earliest applied wall finishes were whitening of the plaster with lime wash, and the oiling of the wood with linseed oil. In the early 1700s some wood walls were painted, and in the smaller houses that paint was often home-made. The colors most often used were a dark red made by mixing Venetian red and lampblack, or a grayish blue of which there are ten known authentic hues. The various gray blues can be duplicated today by tinting white paint with a mixture of chrome green, Chinese blue, and lampblack in varying proportions.

In the Southern colonies the larger houses were painted inside as early as 1727, pearl and cream being the popular colors. After 1745 painted rooms were common both North and South. The Georgian rooms could be a gray, blue-gray, gray-green, or ivory. The grays we can imitate by mixing lampblack with lemon yellow, with lemon yellow and chrome green, or with chrome yellow and chrome green.

In some houses small painted areas were strongly colored a dark violet-red, and the inside of cupboards a bright crimson. In the later classic-style houses which had decorated ceilings in the Adam style, the ceilings sometimes were tinted. The favored colors were yellowish greens, gray-greens, light crimson, blue-greens, pale salmon, and light blue-violet.

In the very early houses fabrics were used at windows, and draped over chests and cupboards, and used for seat cushions. The simplest were homespun woolens, dyed in the purples and reds that the housewife could easily contrive in her fireside dyepot. Later those who could afford such luxuries could obtain damasks, velvets, Turkey work, and crewel embroidery. In a few more years there became available East India prints, painted linens and cottons, needlepoint, calicoes, and chintzes. Any and all of these could be used with oak or walnut furniture.

For the Georgian interiors and their mahogany furniture, the more formal of the foregoing materials were used, together with a variety of new ones—English printed cottons, Colonial hand-blocked prints, imported damasks, brocatelles, reps, serges, and toiles de Jouy.

In the later Classical and Federal Periods, Chinese silks and embroideries were imported, together with satin, taffeta, moiré and plush. Linsey-woolsey, of which clothes were made as well as hangings, was of course a home product used in the smaller and less affluent houses.

The patterns of these later materials were often of the Roman type, large in scale and brilliant in color, with blue, orange, and pink predominating. This information is given merely as a guide and not as a pattern to copy. What we are interested in is recapturing the early atmosphere of these period houses and establishing the character of the rooms. This we can very well do without using exact duplicates of the materials, designs, or patterns. But we *must* select, so far as is possible, fabrics that are enough like the old ones in texture and appearance.

*Two fabrics ideal for the Early American and informal Georgian home:
an 18th Century printed cotton, Williamsburg "Flower and Tassels"
pattern and, below, another Williamsburg design, somewhat less bold.*

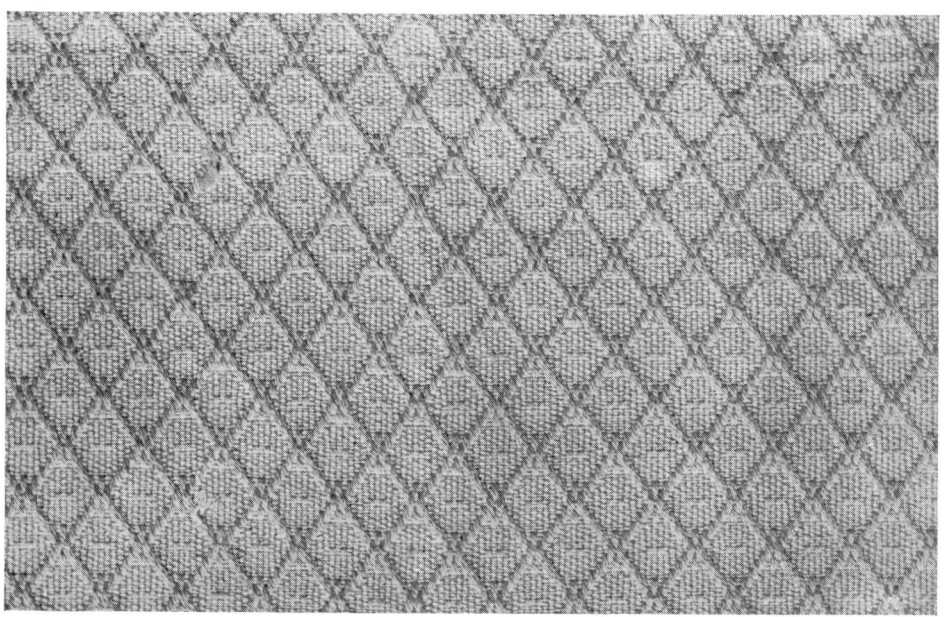

Two excellent simple patterns. At top is a modern fabric with raised thread in solid color, sturdy enough for upholstery use; below it is a reproduction of an old-time homespun fabric in a variety of colors.

A rich, arresting combination of color and design which would go well in either the formal Early American setting or in the Georgian home.

Interesting Shaker fabric in three colors, one of the best of its type.

The modern trend has for a long time been toward the use of pastel shades and diluted colors, and a return to the old positive colors, the primaries, vivid and strong, would be a welcome change. In these early houses we have an excellent opportunity of using plain and restrained backgrounds, sometimes warm like old pumpkin pine or neutral like off-white plaster, as a foil for lively fabrics.

In the earliest rooms we don't need to use Turkey work; there are many acceptable substitutes. Crewel embroidery is always available, though often expensive, for bed hangings and wing chair coverings. Much cheaper and sometimes just as effective are linens printed with the old crewel work designs. For sofas and chairs we can get a host of suitable fabrics ranging from the most formal silk, satin, or velvet, to printed linen. But for most of the Early American small houses, the linen would have to suffice.

When you get into the Georgian era with its polished mahogany there is less objection to the silks and satins, but the simpler domiciles take more kindly to calico prints and chintzes. Cottons help to reduce the extreme formality of some Georgian rooms and emphasize the Colonial feel. Old-fashioned flower patterns are preferable but you can occasionally substitute a good and colorful documentary print provided the period is correct. In small rooms, tiny patterned all-over designs are usually best.

For the classic periods, with Hepplewhite, Sheraton and Phyfe furniture, formal over-all patterns and geometric designs are good, as are some stripes. For the immediate post-Revolutionary period, it is also appropriate to use classic designs of Roman and Greek origin.

In deciding on any of the foregoing materials you have to remember two things: to select a material and pattern representative of the period, and to keep in mind the room you are dealing with. Some materials and patterns that are charming in bedrooms are too inconsequential for living rooms. The purpose of the rooms must therefore be considered and the total areas of fabric and wood in each of them, because this affects their character and the quantity of patterned material you can use.

Wall Decoration

The idea of decorating walls with painted designs seems to have started in America at about the time that wallpapers became popular, i.e. about 1780. Very few decorated walls have been found that can be positively dated before the Revolution. But as far back as the early 1700s paneled walls were painted in two shades of the same color to emphasize the modeling of panels and cornices, though painted designs on the panels were rare. Then, suddenly, it became important to decorate the simple walls of the small house, too.

Seemingly, no one knows how the fashion started, but artists, amateur and professional, got to work cutting stencils. Borders in color were stenciled on white plaster with astonishingly happy results. Bolder spirits paneled the walls with stencil borders, and finally applied all-over designs. Most of the stencil designs were stylized flowers and foliage, but geometric patterns also were used, the favorite colors being reds, browns, and greens. This fashion reached its zenith around 1830. Meanwhile the rage for wallpaper had reached into even the humblest homes.

The first recorded American wallpaper manufacturer was one Plunkett Fleeson, an upholsterer-undertaker of Philadelphia. In 1739, when the 16-by 12-inch sheets of wallpaper were being imported and sold by the quire and ream like writing paper, he started to make his own. History does not record the results, but by 1780 the papers were much cheaper though most were imported from France and China. The sheets then were 30 by 40 inches. Not till ten years later were they manufactured here on a really commercial basis. Even then most small householders could only afford to use the papers as borders. In 1760 some attempt had been made to manufacture longer strips of wallpaper by pasting together two dozen of the smaller sheets before printing them. "Endless" paper was not made till 1799 and improved manufacturing methods had to wait on that.

One of the early uses of wallpaper was to simulate moldings. Walls that had no dado or chair rail were given a paper one. Sometimes the space below the rail would be filled in with marbleized paper, or paper panels. The space above the rail might then be painted in color or papered in separate panels with paper molding strips. Cornices were provided in the same way. So well were the printed moldings drawn and shaded that they were hard to tell from the real thing at a distance. Excellent copies are made of them today.

Another use for the molding papers was to frame panels of patterned paper. This dressed up the walls at less expense than all-over papering, but it is not recommended for use today. Papered panels really do not look well with surrounds of bare plaster. Likewise the well-known scenic wallpapers that were all the rage in 1817 (also obtainable in reproduction today) are not suitable for the small house, besides being expensive, so we can pass them over.

From this brief review of early wall decorations it will no doubt have been gathered that neither stencils nor wall papers would be authentic in small houses much before the Revolution. Nevertheless any older house still existing, and whose rooms need the architectural or decorative help of either paper or painted designs may quite properly have them. Books on authentic stencil designs are available, and many art museums have collections of designs in their files.

Though you may have to employ an artist or designer to make the stencils and do the work for you (unless you are capable of doing it yourself), you will certainly not have such difficulties with wallpaper. Your principal problem there will be to choose the right pattern from the many authentic designs offered by the leading wallpaper manufacturers. But those authentic designs will probably be of papers first designed after 1800. The floral designs will more likely be dated as late as 1840.

As we pointed out earlier, very few rooms can be wholly authentic—except in museum displays—they would not be satisfactory for living in if they were. Rooms that have lived have grown, and it is quite permissible to make later additions of this sort providing you do not destroy the antique air of the room in the process. It is a matter of fact that papering the rooms of small old houses can give them added interest and charm as nothing else can. It may actually intensify the venerable air of age and bring out qualities in the furniture that were lost in a background of white plaster and plain paint. The paper, of course, must be just right; and fortunately it costs little to experiment before taking the final step.

Then, too, there is a very useful type of wall "paper" made of fabric which can be used over old uneven and cracked walls, and may even save a replastering job. It comes in good designs, and has the added advantage of being washable.

Choosing the Paper

Selecting the right pattern of wallpaper to use in any room would be much simpler if we had completely papered rooms as samples. It takes a good deal of imagination to visualize such a room from a two-foot square sample. It also helps if you know something of the principles governing the use of color in a room. This is especially important in connection with wallpapers where we have both color and pattern combined.

One easily remembered principle is that light colors make a room seem larger; dark ones have the opposite effect. Likewise blue tints increase the apparent size and red tints reduce it. Here wallpaper has the advantage over paint. You can get plenty of red colors into a room without making the room seem smaller through the use of red-patterned wallpaper, provided the pattern is well-spaced over a light background.

If you have a paper with a small, widely scattered design on a white or light background you will get a feeling of space. If the pattern is large and crowded it will close in on you. Any paper whose design has perspective will, on the contrary, push back the walls. Conversely, papers patterned with large, solid blocks of color draw the walls together.

We are not in a position to know whether or not our 18th century ancestors knew these things, but it is certain that they experimented with effects. Quite a few old rooms were papered on adjoining walls, and the other two walls left bare. We therefore have precedent for the decorator's trick of papering one wall only or facing walls to draw those walls together, or apparently push them farther apart.

In the old houses this is often a useful idea. For example you may have a room that is paneled at one end and plain plaster at the other. Or you may have one that has several windows in one wall and a large, unbroken expanse opposite—one in the light and one in the shadow! In such instances the furniture may not be sufficient to give a feeling of balance to the room. Using an unobtrusive wallpaper on the shadowy broken-up wall and a strongly patterned one on the other may set things right.

Other principles that you need to bear in mind in choosing the paper concern the suitability of the pattern to a room. Small rooms as a rule look better with a paper that contains little color contrast and has a small design. Larger rooms on the contrary can often stand large or bold patterns. In the latter case you have to use discrimination because our old-time rooms are rarely overlarge. Usually it is better to treat the walls in such a manner that the room neither shrinks nor expands. If the paper tends to shrink the room you can often counteract that effect by using either a contrasting dado, or a wide border or frieze at the ceiling. This seems to balance the room by making it seem lower, and therefore longer and wider in proportion to the height. Incidentally, most of the early wallpapers made use of the border.

The third important principle is to select a paper that will combine with the furniture to create the kind of personality you want the room to have. A formally furnished room can look slightly silly with an overgay and sprightly paper background. Likewise the bedroom of an active young male appears somewhat out of key with a delicate pattern.

Luckily there are a great many reproductions of old papers on the market, and many more new designs inspired by them. Among the most popular of the early designs are those known as stencil patterns. These designs actually look as though they had been stenciled on the paper. The background paper may be of any color or none at all.

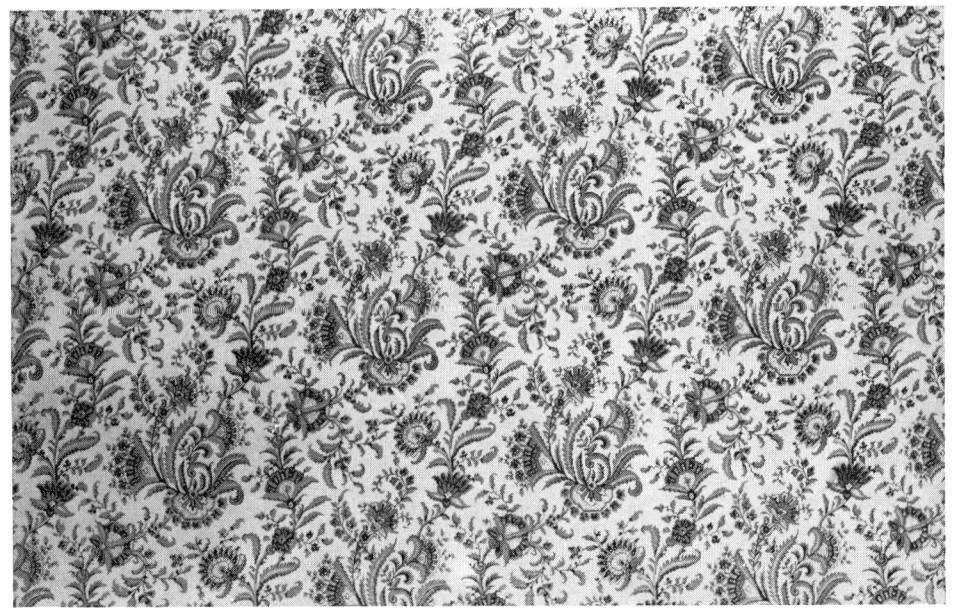

Dainty floral wallpaper, top, in delicate colors especially suited to bedroom-dressing room use; below, a rich all-over pattern with an Oriental feeling to dramatize whatever room it graces.

This colorful semi-formal pattern, predominantly floral, is well suited to the more simple Georgian hall, living room or bed chamber.

A good pattern for the large formal room with much light-colored wood-work. Can be used in hall, living room or bedroom successfully.

Stencil wallpapers such as this require careful introduction to a room as they eliminate other wall decoration, and call for selective choice of fabrics and floor coverings. Properly used, it is most effective.

A Greek Revival or Federal paper in dark, rich colors.

Good example of a documentary wallpaper design, of which there is now a large selection. This was copied from a house in Marblehead, Mass.

Interesting snow-crystal pattern in white with neutral gray background.

The stencil patterns, like the printed ones, need to be chosen for their effect. Some have a lacy feel, especially those printed in white or cream on a colored background. Many of them have circular designs inside a pattern of square borders so that they happily combine formality with frills.

Papers for the Georgian and Federal houses are legion. The Georgian designs lean heavily toward the figured and pictorial patterns, and all-over florals. The more classic periods are well taken care of with geometrical, domino, and classical patterns such as honeycomb frames, panels, and vases of somewhat stylized flowers.

For rooms furnished with Chinese Chippendale pieces you can have brilliant reproductions of tea papers. There are many to choose from in reds and golds with green foliage, or Chinese pastoral papers in gold and silver and vivid greens on a red background, and even bamboo and geometrical designs. Most of the leading wallpaper makers stock papers specially designed for Chippendale rooms, but the number of suitable Georgian papers is almost endless. The list includes a great variety of French colonial designs, many of them pastorals, or flowers framed in intricate and sinuous moldings. For the small house, though, your selection is somewhat limited because so many of the designs are suited only to large or formal rooms.

For the Federal or Greek Revival houses any of the vertically striped Regency papers are suitable. But never should you use the very modern horizontally striped papers. If you need a horizontal line effect you can perhaps use one of the oblong tile or panel patterns called block designs.

If your house is furnished in the Hepplewhite style you can get flock papers decorated with that designer's characteristic motive—if you like flock papers. Many do not. Other classical types are the diaper and medallion combinations and some domino designs.

Small Early American style houses naturally call for unpretentious papers, but it is extraordinary how broad a field that covers. Particularly suitable are dainty chintz papers, and the exquisite toiles de Jouy which look as though they were printed on fabric. The toiles, however, should not be of the architectural type adorned with ruined castles and Roman pillars. The most amenable designs are the all-over, thread-like patterns, especially in red or blue on a white background. But we have not seen one that is not tidy and in good taste. A particularly beautiful effect is secured with some chintz patterns by embossing the paper so that it looks and feels like quilting.

Washable wall covering, available in a variety of bleached tones, simulating wood. Useful in library, den, living room, hall, game room.

The plain, paneled walls of this room make an excellent foil for the Gulistan carpet fashioned from an authentic Colonial needlework pattern. An excellent choice for the Colonial or Victorian setting.

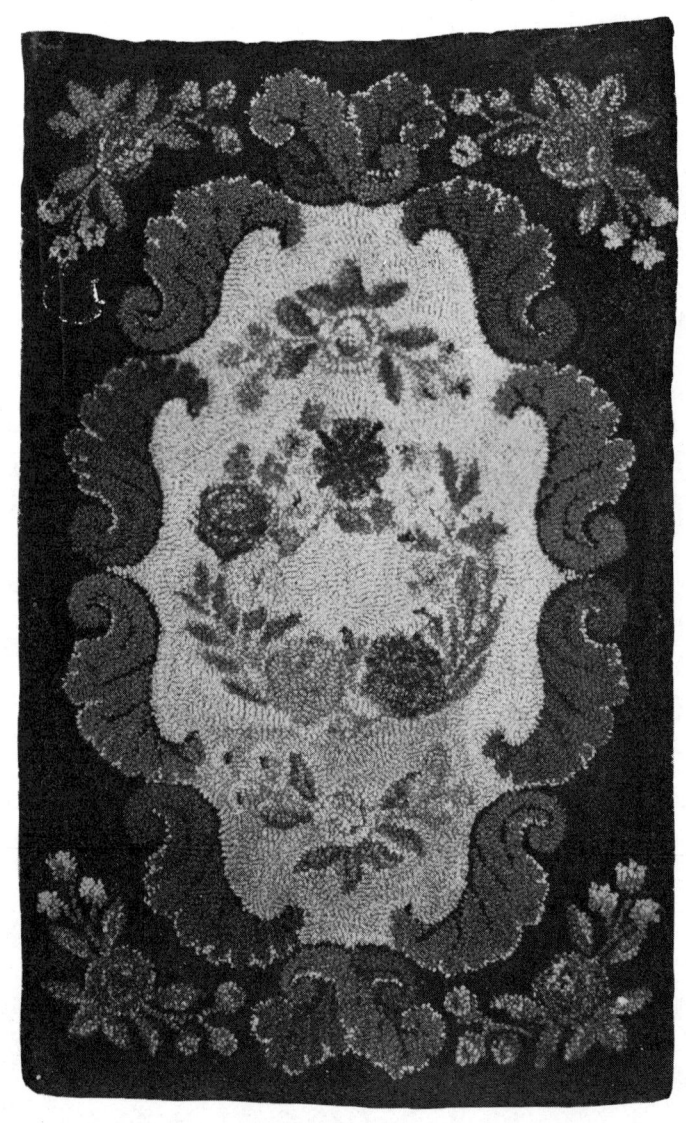

Hooked rug of pleasing color and design in dark, strong colors.

In contrast to the preceding illustration, the plain fiber floor covering of this room tones down the wallpaper and fabrics. Dark furniture and an abundance of white also help neutralize color and texture.

Delicate-patterned hooked rug especially suited to bedroom use.

Floor Treatments

It often happens that one of the most interesting features of an old-time room is the floor. The wide oak or pine boards, worn by generations of busy feet, and mopped and oiled for many a decade, have a character that only time and natural wear can give. In the more fashionable houses these wide boards may have been looked upon as primitive crudities and replaced with the much more *raffinée* narrow matched boards, or even covered with modern flooring.

You are lucky indeed if you still have the old floors and they have not had all the character sanded out of them. In the small houses particularly they contribute vastly to the old-time appearance and blend with almost any but the strictly formal furniture styles. In the larger houses, and those of Georgian style, the wide board floors are often equally effective, especially when the large expanse is broken up by rugs so that the effect is not overpowering.

The exposed wide boards do sometimes have the effect of making a room seem narrow, but in small rooms there is generally not enough of them visible to make much difference when the furniture is in place. As a general rule it is a good thing to leave the old floor boards exposed and take advantage of their atmospheric qualities. In the case of newly built Colonials, or with floors that are too badly worn and uneven, it is often best to cover them up.

The modern wide-board floors, planed, sanded, and all-too-obviously pegged, do little to establish an air of antiquity. They are too much like stage props and the less seen of them the better. A glimpse here and there of their pristine surfaces will be far more convincing than total exposure.

Colored Floors

In the latter part of the 18th century it became a common practice to paint floors. The most popular colors were gray, dark green, gray-green in various combinations, pumpkin yellow, chocolate brown, and a delightful terra cotta red. Sometimes the whole floor was painted and at others only a border.

A somewhat later development was the stenciled floor. Often this was reserved for the best rooms and perhaps the bedrooms. The stencil patterns were occasionally used as borders to the painted floors, but in many instances the border was all that was painted. Both geometric and stylized flower and leaf stencil designs were used. On some painted floors decorations were

This Colonial tile-effect carpet has a warm, inviting air.

added by stenciling a small design such as a flower or a star at large intervals all over it. Any one of these ideas can be adopted with profit when the condition or character of the floor warrants it.

A floor finish with a quaint but much less Colonial air is the so-called spatter painting. This appears to have originated around 1840, but it does contribute an old-fashioned feel to a room—provided it is done properly. Amateur attempts at spatter painting are often a sad failure, but everyone seems to think he can do it. Briefly, it consists of splashing small spots of various colored paints over a floor that has previously been painted a solid background color, usually dark.

Floor Coverings

In recent years the vogue for Colonial and Early American furnishing has encouraged manufacturers to produce floor coverings for old-time settings. Furthermore, some of the newer materials, such as cork and plastic tile, are proving adaptable to old-time rooms. Whether or not to lay down "permanent" floor covering such as linoleum, depends on circumstances—and the room. In bathrooms and kitchens and in many hallways, linoleum and similar materials have distinct advantages. For one thing they are easy to keep clean, and in addition help to insulate the floors of downstairs rooms.

Even upstairs such materials can help insulate the old floors against noise. But it is important to choose the right kind of material and the proper pattern or no pattern at all. If you cannot have the original wood floor surface on which to use scatter rugs of various sorts, the next best thing in all secondary rooms is good quality linoleum or tile.

Included in the waterproof floor covering materials that we recommend are cork tiles. For many locations they are preferable to other materials simply because of their close resemblance to wood. Apart from this, they are undoubtedly one of the most satisfactory floorings for old houses that we have encountered. They are moisture-proof, skid-proof, and never feel cold to the touch. Naturally they must be properly applied and laid level. But if you get your cork flooring from a reputable maker you will have something that looks well and feels as well as it looks. The cork tiles come in a variety of sizes and shapes so that old-time floorings can be simulated. Some colors match the old oak boards or the lighter old pine, and browner shades are obtainable so that interesting pattern combinations can be worked out. The only place where cork flooring is not advisable is in the kitchen. Grease-proof asphalt tile or linoleum in colors to represent old tiles or boards are better there. Linoleum and tile patterns are discussed later.

An unusual geometric carpet pattern for use in the Federal room.

This rich floral pattern would look well in most Georgian living rooms.

In the realm of movable floor coverings, and suitable to the old houses are the various old-style rugs and carpets. The first Colonial floor coverings were sand and rushes. In the Southern mansions, floor carpets were imported in the 17th century, but in the less well-to-do homes, the materials known as carpets were used on beds and furniture.

The earliest form of made floor covering in America, subsequent to the use of skins, dating back to the 17th century, appears to have been the forerunner of linoleum. It was a floor-sized sheet of canvas, painted, usually, in large black and white squares. Such coverings or carpets appear in many paintings of Dutch Colonial interiors of that period. But in the smaller Colonial homes large and small carpets apparently were not often encountered before the middle of the 18th century. At that time other portrait paintings show patterned carpeting. It was about this time that trade with the Orient was booming, and oriental rugs from China, the East Indies and India were imported in large quantities by shipowners and the gentry for their own use.

In the more modest homes, small rugs of braided rushes, and later of cloth strips or rags undoubtedly were used. The hooked rug was introduced very late in the 18th century. This type of rug apparently originated in Scandinavia some hundreds of years ago, and came to the colonies through England as well as the Scandinavian settlements.

A striking pattern with a decidedly Federal or Greek Revival air.

With homespun materials and home-made dyes, some very beautiful though primitive examples were produced in these early days. Flowers, animals, and mottoes were used as patterns of which the all-over flower designs were probably the most delightful.

In the 19th century manufacturers sold burlap with designs stenciled on so that the rug makers had no need to design their own. As a result the products became stereotyped and uninteresting and generally quite ugly. Today the art of hooked rug making has been somewhat revived, and individual designs are again available.

In the better Colonial homes before the Revolution, rugs of cross-stitch and needlework were occasionally made and used in bedrooms and boudoirs.

The only other kind of rug developed at this time was the rag rug, either woven into burlap backing or sewn into strips and braided. Today the braided rugs, if hand-made of carefully selected materials, cannot be excelled for the small Colonial house.

In these modest homes the large or overall carpet was practically unknown till the middle of the 19th century, but in the homes of the wealthy every kind of large rug and carpet was used, from Aubussons to Axminsters.

9

RUSHLIGHTS TO STUDENT LAMPS: *Early forms of light-ing—Modern lighting—Electric "candles"—Table lamps and shades—What is a lamp base?*

In today's Colonial houses illumination is almost a part of the furnish-ing, with boundless opportunities for anachronisms in lighting fixtures and consequent loss of authentic air. In the early days our first colonists either went to bed with the setting sun or made out with the light of a fire. Later in the 17th century they made wooden "candles" out of pitch pine slivers or soaked rushes in fat and called them rushlights.

The first lamps were shallow tins of whale oil in which a dab of moss served as a wick. These iron dishes were known as betty lamps and provided the room with more smell and smoke than light. Still later the colonists melted beef tallow and molded the soft fat with their fingers around wick strings to form candles. The first lighting fixtures, then, were rushlight holders, betty lamps, candle sconces, candlesticks and trammels, candle stands and chandeliers. All of these were used more or less indiscriminately till well into the 18th century.

By that time every housewife knew how to refine fats and make hard candles that were not quite so odorous as the tallow ones. They used vege-table wax from bayberry plants, sheep suet, and beeswax, and by 1730 got spermaceti from whale oil. With less smoky candles they could use more of them in a room without coating everyone and everything with soot.

Some concentration of light was secured by the use of wood or metal wall sconces and reflectors, and room lighting effected with wood and metal chandeliers holding two to a dozen candles. In rooms with very low ceilings it was not possible to use a chandelier without burning down the house, and the candles had to be held in floor stands.

When glass chimneys were invented in 1783 the so-called "hurricane" globe became popular for table lighting and protecting candles placed on tables and sideboards and mantels from drafts. So many of those lighting devices can be adapted to present-day use that it is a pity not to take advantage of them in furnishing period rooms.

Possibly the only one of these devices that has neither utility or appearance to recommend it is the rushlight holder. The originals often were made of a heavy wrought iron bar, bent and hinged so that it formed a pair of jaws. The weight of the iron kept the jaws closed and clamped on the rush light. A rough block of wood may have served as a base, though floor stands, and spikes for jabbing into the woodwork also were used.

The iron candle holders were made along the same lines but had thin iron sockets for the candles. Consequently they were much less ungainly. Probably the only type of candle holder that we cannot use today would be the adjustable wooden trammel by which the candle could be hung at various heights from the ceiling beams, the back of the settle, or a fireplace lintel. Incidentally, many a lintel had a long wooden swinging arm attached to it with a candle socket at the end. This could be swung out into the room in front of a settle or alongside a chair for the benefit of readers or writers.

Much more decorative than any of these were the wall sconces. Often home-made, they might consist of little wooden shelves with fragmentary sides to curtail drafts, and a metal cup to hold the candle. More ambitious home craftsmen bent and crimped oblong pieces of thin iron plate and bent up the lower end to form a shelf and candle socket. Even those of the 17th century were of interesting shapes, usually tall and narrow, and perhaps with a semi-circular crown. Sometimes an attempt was made to polish them and later on iron ones were made with bits of looking glass let in as reflectors.

Other sconces of more professional design contained large pieces of mirror made to look as though they were framed. More expensive types were made of pewter or Sheffield plate or even solid silver, but painted tôle ware or japanned iron were more common. In some instances circular sconces were favored. These had saucer-shaped reflectors, either polished or lined with many small sections of mirrored glass.

Ordinary candlesticks were made of wood, pewter, brass, and japanned iron as well as silver and, later, Sheffield plate. Very few silver candlesticks were made in the colonies. The colonial silversmiths preferred to concentrate on other things, but many china and pottery ones were turned out before 1800.

The metal floor-type candle stands were much like modern bridge

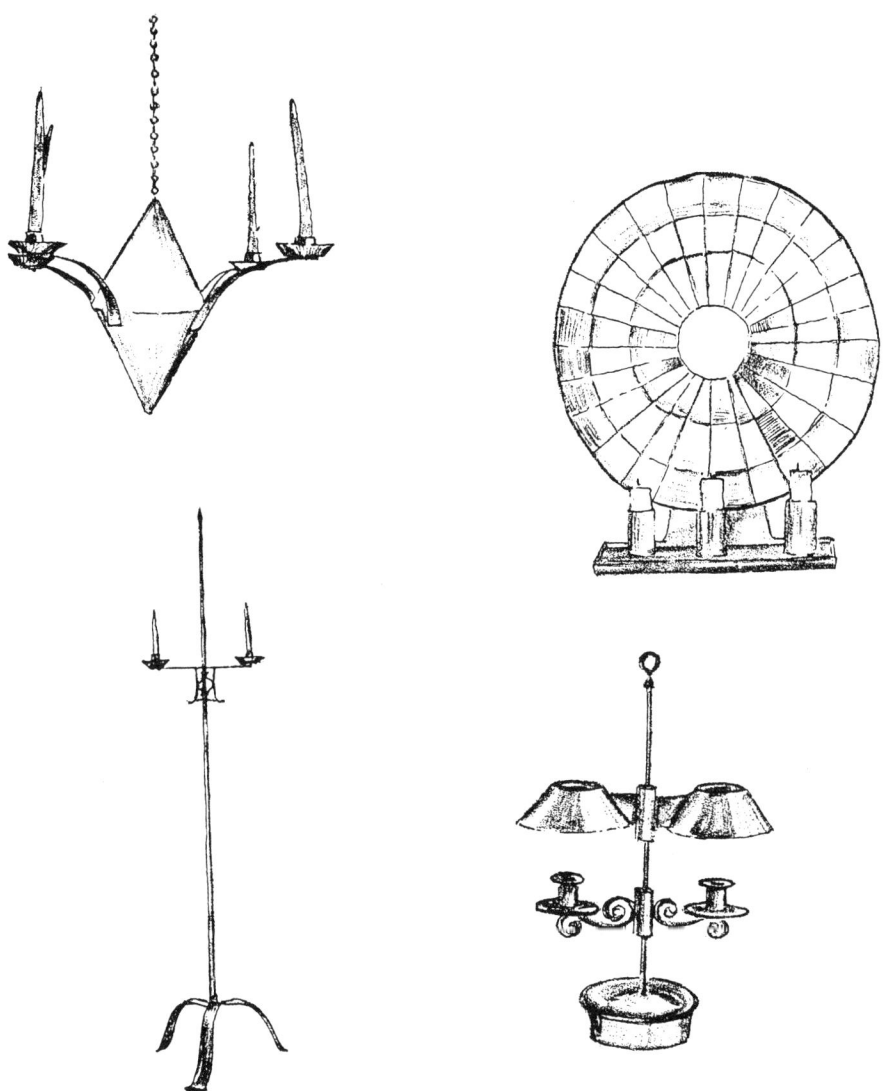

Early types of lighting fixtures easily adapted to modern living.

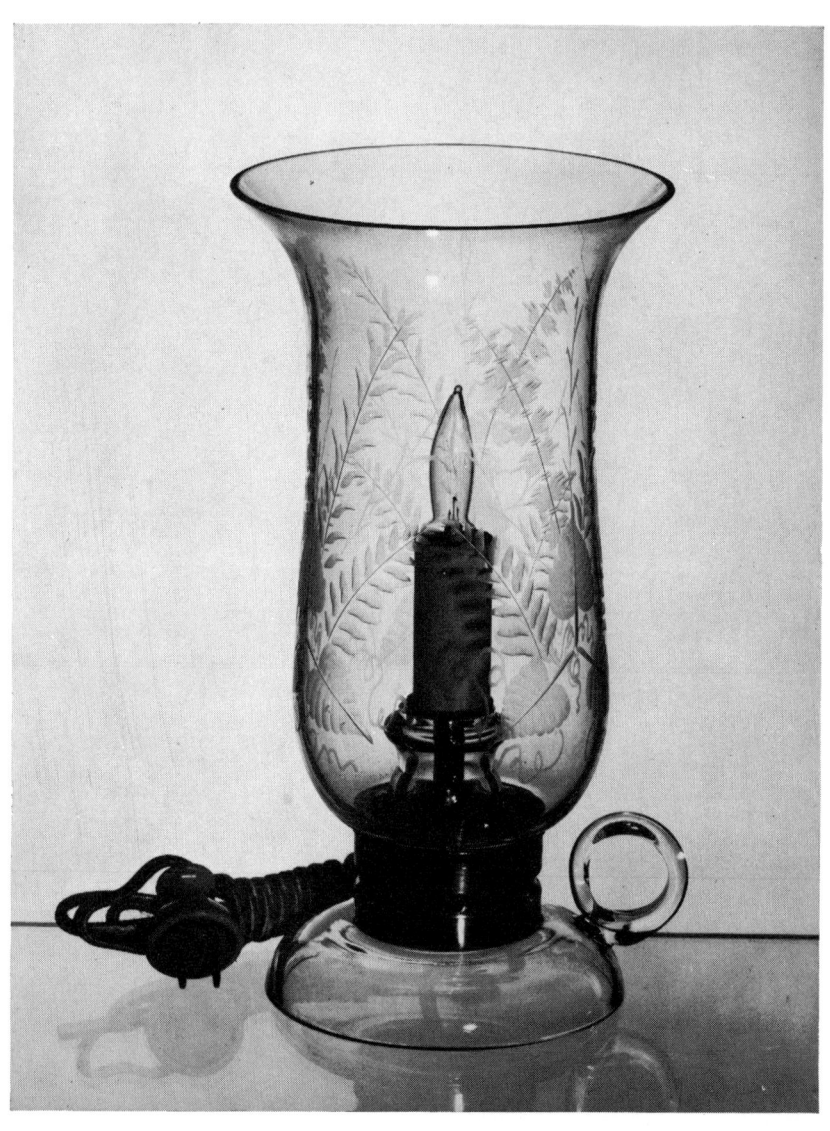

Modern adaptation of the old "hurricane" candle-holder with electric simulated candle, a style suited to use in almost every room in the house.

lamps in shape, but often more graceful because they did not need to be so heavy. The upright iron spindle, mounted on three or four branching legs was usually quite slender and sometimes tapering. The sliding cross bar that held one or two candles, was held in position on the spindle by a curved flat spring that was both effective and decorative.

The wooden stands were of two types. The most graceful were the tall variety consisting of a pedestal support with a small circular table top. In the other type practically all had an upright spindle threaded like a screw. The arms that held the candles could be raised or lowered by winding them up or down the screw. This kind of stand was first made in walnut, cherry, or maple. Later on much finer ones were produced in mahogany.

The ordinary table candlestick was a common object in early 18th century homes, and special small tables were made to hold them. These tables were placed in the hallways or entries, or other nooks close to the stairs as a convenience for people ascending to the upper floors after dark. There would of course be a lighted candle on the table from which the other could be lit. This practice still survives in some country homes. Eighteenth century card tables had corner pieces, often dished, to hold the candlesticks, and secretaries were fitted with sliding flaps for the same purpose.

Early chandeliers were often weird and intricate affairs. Huge wooden turnings supported thin iron arms, octopus fashion, on the ends of which perched the candles. Other chandeliers were made entirely of metal, with a dozen or more candles mounted on an oblong dished base, with perhaps a metal hood to deflect the heat from the ceiling. In the more elaborate houses it was not long before the chandeliers were the most decorative feature of a room.

Intricate, many-tiered chandeliers of crystal and colored Venetian glass were imported from France and Italy, but most people were content with hanging lanterns and hanging lamps, or the simple candle beam—an iron cross or ring with four or more candles disposed at intervals. Even in the first quarter of the 18th century many houses had hanging candle lamps in the entry or hall.

In the Georgian houses, mantels and tables were adorned with candelabra festooned with crystal prisms and decorative gilt metal ornaments. In Federal houses candelabra of a little more classical design were used. They also had lamps with glass shades supported on columns.

During all this time the only real advance in lighting was the invention of the Argand lamp in 1783. The handicap to any real progress was of course the lack of suitable fuel. Kerosene was not used for lamps till 1880.

The Argand lamp however really did give a good light. It had a tubular wick and air was admitted inside the ring of flame as well as outside it. But whale oil lamps were in use long before then, some with one wick, some with two or three. Later on came the lard-oil lamps and camphine (alcohol and turpentine) lamps. But none of these is likely to be used in a modern house. Candles, it is to be hoped, will be used for a long time to come.

Modern Lighting

Even in these progressive United States there are still houses where electricity is not installed, and the people in them live as happy and contented lives as those to whom this boon is extended. But we certainly cannot quarrel with anyone who prefers electric lighting even in an antique house. Anyone who has spent half a day several times a week cleaning and filling oil lamps will understand what we mean. To anyone living a modern life that adjunct to modern living is no mere luxury but a necessity. Therefore, even at the expense of a little atmosphere in our old-time houses, we are indubitably better off with electric lights. As a matter of fact, if you exercise a little care in your selection of lighting equipment very little will be lost. Then, too, you do not altogether need to forfeit the attractions of candlelight. In even the most sophisticated and modern homes the light of a candle is only second to an open fire in its appeal to the sentimental side of our natures. Indeed no form of illumination is so soft and kindly, or so romantic as the mellow glow of candlelight.

Candles *do* belong in the Old American house but not for reading by or doing any of the things that tax the eyes. They provide sufficient light for the dinner table, and decoration as well, and as an accompaniment to conversation or music. Even when unlit they constitute an ornament with a useful purpose. But candles need attention, and the hazard of fire always accompanies an open flame. For this reason many people substitute imitation candles that are really electric lights.

In wall sconces these dummy candles are particularly effective, but only if they duplicate the yellow candle flame. The common torch flame light bulbs are neither attractive nor in good.taste. Sconces are obtainable in seemingly endless variety, from a simple metal leaf to the round web mirror type. In selecting a sconce for an old-time room you need to choose an authentic design and not a modern gift-shop item.

There are on the market some long, slender electric candles for use in wired candelabra. They have a tiny "flame" light and are therefore effective, provided you don't get too close to them. Under certain conditions,

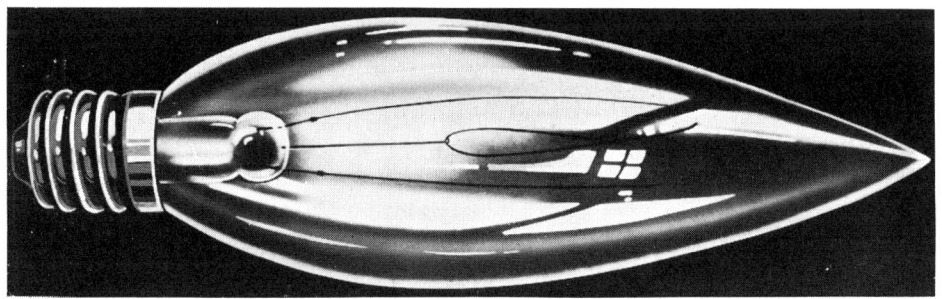

A type of electric light bulb that gives the effect of a candle flame.

however, they look affected and a little too sophisticated. Therefore you need to use them with care and not in too prominent positions. The type made of mirrored glass should of course be entirely avoided. In chandeliers where the bulbs cannot be seen the small lights that give a yellow glow can be used effectively.

Because of the deficiencies of the ordinary electric bulb for old-fashioned interiors it is generally better to disguise them in electrified oil lamps and lanterns. These look more natural than the naked imitation candles, and reproductions of old-style pieces are made for almost any purpose or location.

For small-house kitchens the popular ceiling light is one with a conical metal shade and glass lamp chimney simulating the early whale-oil type. For dining rooms you can have simple old-style chandeliers with anywhere from two to five lights, each having its own metal shade. The simpler these are, the more effective and less obtrusive in the Old American room.

Student lamps are a 19th century development, but a delightful one! They look well in Georgian or even Federal surroundings as well as in Early American or Victorian. One successful adaptation that we like particularly is the double student lamp, minus its base, suspended by a brass rod from the ceiling so that it serves as a chandelier (electrified, of course).

Table Lamps and Shades

And so at last we come to the perennial subject of table lamps and the touchy matter of lamp bases. Lamps are beloved of amateur decorators for their "accent" value both day and night. Nothing is too odd or too eccentric an object for a lamp base. As long as it will hold a socket and shade, anything will do, from an old riding boot to a butter churn.

In our opinion these pieces should be reserved for modern interiors where everything is designed for drama, to shock, to amuse, to entertain— or constitute a conversation piece! Our old-time houses, we feel, should be reserved to the proper functions of a home, and not emulate a waxworks. At any rate, the deciding factor in the choice of a lamp should be whether or not it adds to or detracts from the antique air and old-fashioned charm.

There is also the important question of good taste. We do not think that kitchen utensils (any more than bedroom utensils) or milk-shed gadgets however old and quaint should be used in the other rooms of the house. Admittedly, this is a subject on which it is difficult to generalize because some old-time objects, no longer suited to or required for the purpose for which they were made, do lend themselves handsomely to other uses. One of our prize possessions, for example, is a lamp made from an early 19th century wooden mortar. We do not find it objectionable because the mortar is a nicely turned, finely patinaed wooden object that might well have been

The 19th Century student lamp, electrified, at home in the old-fashioned rooms of almost any period. Single and double styles are equally popular.

made for a lamp base in the beginning. For that reason it is *not* an object that bears absolutely no relation to its present use, nor one that will never look like anything but what it is. And that, we think, should be the criterion.

We do not see that a metal coffee grinder with an electric light standard protruding from its vitals is either an object of beauty or of suitability to a room of antique charm. These are the reasons why we consider that adapted lamp bases should be confined to objects that look natural in that rôle. Certain pieces of old pottery, glassware, pewter, tôle, and woodware fill the bill nicely. Many a beautiful lamp has been made from ginger jars, certain old bottles, china figurines, tea canisters, and so on.

Often of greater importance than the lamp bases in room decoration are the lamp shades. These cannot contribute much to the antique air of a room, but the materials from which they are made and their decoration can certainly help. The shades can either spoil the entire effect of a room or supply just that touch that brings a room to life and sets the seal on its character.

In the small old house it is a good plan to have the lamp shades take their color and perhaps their pattern from the wallpaper, upholstery fabrics, or hangings. Where this is not possible, or as an alternative, their background color should match that of some important feature of the room. Where there are several lamps in one room it is advisable to have all the shades more or less alike, but do not decide on any color or pattern until you have seen it with the lamp lit in a darkened room as well as in the daylight.

This modern adaptation of a whale-oil hanging lamp adds charms and authenticity to old-time kitchens.

Unsophisticated shades, which is what the simple house needs, especially with pine paneling and pine or walnut furniture, can be of paper decorated or plain. If the paper shades are decorated it should be with a simple, old-time pattern. Chintz is equally good, or even paper with a chintz pattern appliqued on it. Stenciled patterns on paper need very careful selection to get the right degree of formality. Lamps with tôle shades, which of course are better for reading than general illumination, can be used in both formal and informal rooms. But those made with golden arrows for arms or other classical motives should be reserved for Phyfe or Empire rooms.

For a Georgian atmosphere the lampshades on the taller lamps can be of some opaque material because enough light will escape to cover a fairly large area. These shades may be highly colored, and glazed on the outside. For more classic interiors gold or silver decoration in Greek or Roman designs are in order. In a great many Georgian rooms lamps with engraved glass shades are used, but to our eyes these generally look Victorian. Much more in keeping are simple, rather severe parchment shades, either plain or with a formal decoration. Alternatively you can use a fabric shade of formal shape which will give the tinted glow that adds interest to any room. Even silk shades will do provided they are smooth, not pleated, and are bound with plain edging. The edging however may be of a contrasting color. For rooms done in Chinese Chippendale there are available many designs of Chinese figurine lamps with shades suggestive of pagoda roofs, or conical shades with a slight inward curve to the sides.

Bedroom lamp shades, whatever the period, can be of plain material but adorned with frills, or of plain design ornamented with decorative swags. Some prefer shades made from the room wallpaper, or with the wallpaper design pasted on a paper base. Whatever type is used it is good to tie it in with one of the colors used elsewhere in the room.

IO

HARLEQUINS TO CLOCKS: *Double-purpose furniture—Kitchen pieces in the living room—New uses for old things—Built-in units—Things hanging on walls—Other framed items—Old timepieces.*

One of Thomas Sheraton's happiest faculties was that of designing pieces of furniture that were a good deal more than they appeared to be. Two examples of this "harlequin" furniture that may well be used in today's homes are, ostensibly, tables.

One is what appears to be a writing table with a top in three sections. When the outer leaves are raised the center portion is automatically lifted, disclosing a compartment fitted with toilet articles. In modern reproductions of this piece the compartment is often equipped as a cellarette.

In the other seemingly innocent table, lifting the top unfolds a pair of library steps complete with handrail. Both of these pieces are useful as well as interesting, and this type of Jekyll and Hyde furniture, with its space-saving advantages, is in perfect taste. But this cannot always be said of the modern tendency to clutter old houses with domestic appliances of the 18th and 19th centuries—objects which serve no visible purpose but to catch dust.

Of course if you are a collector of old Americana there is some excuse for cluttering the hearth with old soup ladles and foot warmers. But the well-dressed room of Colonial and post-Colonial days can look like what it is supposed to be without these artificial aids.

Another tendency to be guarded against is that of adapting certain old-time objects to uses for which they were never intended—and in particular cheap modern reproductions of such objects. In any room that is well and tastefully furnished there surely should be no place for such absurdities as cobblers' benches doubling as coffee tables, milk churns as living room floor lamps, or an infant's cradle stuffed with foliage as a hall decoration! These are frivolous fads on a par with the use of carriage or hearse lamps for front door lights, or spinning wheels on the hearth for atmosphere.

These strictures do not of course apply to every new application of an old piece of furniture. Quite a few articles have, in the course of years, graduated from the kitchen to the living room, and vice versa. And their obvious utility combined with their pleasing appearance justify the move. But there must be some standard by which we can judge the validity of their inclusion in our furnishing schemes.

In all our old-time rooms we must maintain an air of appropriateness and sincerity. Things must not be done for cheap effect. Decorated sadirons used as bookends and door stops are typical affectations to be avoided, except in the country lodge or the most informal of informal rooms where almost anything goes.

For one thing, their original associations have a great deal to do with the fitness of these objects for a new rôle. In the gay nineties a lot of really gorgeous brass cuspidors were made, but few would consider using the finest hammered brass piece as a flower holder today. We have to think of this aspect of adaptation in connection with quite a few items over which antique collectors go into ecstasies.

One of these is that refugee from the milk-house—the milk bench. Now this strictly utilitarian item, which is usually nothing but an old pine shelf with perhaps a couple of cupboards and a small drawer, has no place in either a kitchen or a living room, yet they are among the most sought-after pieces for just those locations. Undoubtedly one reason for this is that the milk bench can be nicely refinished so that it retains little evidence of its humble origin. Inside the house it becomes merely a useful shelf or cupboard, perhaps of somewhat primitive construction but nevertheless an interesting antique.

The same thing can be said of some water benches and dry sinks, and even of the old dough trough or kneading trough whose purpose is generally much more obvious. The dough troughs with a suitable lid do make useful tables and the interior offers storage space though you do have to take everything off the top to get at it. In each case these items do look better in the kitchen than elsewhere, and in fact they do more for that room than any other piece we can think of.

Here it seems that the factor by which we should judge the suitability or otherwise of a primitive piece is its adaptability, and the ease and completeness with which its original purpose can be submerged in a new function. One piece of equipment that does not meet this requirement, and which

The Welsh dresser, used originally in the old kitchen, has been promoted to the dining room for china display and linen storage, or to the living room for books and other accessories.

has the further disadvantage of being extremely unattractive even in a kitchen is the early Victorian food safe with punched tin doors!

In quite another category is the Welsh dresser or Welsh cupboard. This is essentially a kitchen unit, but today many of them are found in living rooms, or even in studies and libraries where they double as book cases.

Some manufacturers of reproduction furniture list what they call hutch cupboards. These are something like a small Welsh dresser—shelves above, cupboards below. The term "hutch" comes from the French "*huche*" which means a kneading trough or bin. Hutches therefore have lids, not doors, so the name hutch cupboard for this piece of furniture is a misnomer. However the cupboard is very like a water bench in appearance, and we find it used both in kitchens and living rooms for a variety of purposes. But the fact remains that we do not have to rely on such pieces to create an atmosphere of antiquity, and often they take away more than they add.

Two intrinsically attractive items that have found their way from the bedroom into the parlor are the wig stand and the basin stand, pieces that are often mistaken for one another and for something else. The wig stand we have seen advertised as a "whig" stand which presumably places it in the same category as a political soap box!

In walnut or mahogany, both stands are graceful pieces of furniture but the basin stand is undoubtedly the most useful—unless one has a toupée! The basin ring, supported on three slender, delicately curved legs can very well hold a copper, brass, or cranberry glass plant or flower container. The little drawers below may be convenient repositories for small items like cigarettes, matches, playing cards, and so forth. The wig stand, which may or may not have the same drawers, must otherwise rely on its decorative value to justify its intrusion. It calls for a great deal of ingenuity to disguise and beautify the naked skull-pan top!

To turn for a moment to a much cruder class of furniture, one outdoor item that does have justification for indoor use is the wagon seat. In the old days they used them in the kitchen when they were not needed for the drive into town. In that room therefore the old wagon seats are quite at home, as they are in the entrance hall of an informal or country dwelling.

Quite a different problem from any of the foregoing is posed by the modern need for coffee tables. This table is purely a 20th century innovation, but although it is an anachronism, it does not need to look out of place in any room. It is merely an extra-low table, and cutting down the height of that piece of furniture does not necessarily involve any other changes or detract from its period air.

The old-time basin stand with its open, ring top is here converted into an attractive plant holder; drawers serve as storage for small items.

It is therefore quite in order to use any coffee table in a room provided the style is the same, or compatible with, the rest of the furniture. Fortunately a great many of these tables are made in readily recognizable period styles. There is also one whose style is not so obvious, yet which is in keeping with various old furniture styles. That is the butler's tray mounted on a stand.

The average coffee table is 18 or 19 inches high. Some people find this a little too low, especially with the bulky overstuffed sofas that give a high seat. They might be able to use one of the smaller tea tables which were made as low as 25 inches.

In the Early Colonial, Jacobean, or William-and-Mary rooms, it is possible to use a joint stool in place of the coffee table, or a reproduction of one of these stools with a longer top. And finally it is strange how well the painted tinware trays of the early 19th century blend in with many old furniture styles. Such a tray, mounted on an iron stand, makes an excellent coffee table without being spoiled for its prime purpose.

One old piece of furniture that fascinates many people who have no real use for it, is a pair of library steps, or even the steps that great-grandfather used for climbing into his mountainous feather bed. These steps nowadays are used in any room at all. Some types are used as end tables for sofas, as night tables, as etagères for the display of curios. Pairs of them, back to back, serve as cocktail tables, and, strangely enough, they are also used as library steps.

The kind of steps that form a box with the upper step for a lid are often used for storage and kept at the foot of the bed. That type, especially those of cruder construction, do not add anything to any room but a bedroom.

Another accessory piece that wanders from the kitchen to other parts of the house is the spice chest—that assembly of three to a dozen or more tiny drawers made to hang on a wall or rest on a shelf. Rarely are they used for their original purpose, and more are found in sewing rooms, or as living room wall decorations than elsewhere. But there can be no denying that they have a great deal of eye-appeal and are among the least objectionable of adapted pieces whether fitted with legs as a sewing stand or used as a bracket for a clock.

Reversing the process and carrying a living room item into the kitchen, hanging shelves can be employed for new purposes. The shelves made for books or bric-a-brac (i.e. dust-catchers) are both interesting and useful over kitchen sinks and counters. But of course they should not be of the pierced or fretwork type, or Chippendale mahogany. We are speaking of the early type shelves of pine or maple or even walnut, with the solid ends. They may or may not have drawers.

It is sometimes a good idea to tack a frill or ruffle to each shelf edge (except the bottom one of course) to keep out dust. Two or three of these shelves hung side by side are effective in appearance, convenient in location,

It is now possible to obtain cabinets for radio and television sets in period styles. Here is a "Salem" chest in modern dress.

Two informal radio cabinets for the Early American room.

These mahogany cabinets are suited to the more formal room.

Small period tables, here shown in modern setting, are always useful in the living room. Plain, pile carpet hides objectionable floors well.

and provide a lot of shelf space without making the room look smaller. In an old-time kitchen they are much more attractive than the modern, closed, blank-faced cupboards.

Small chests, whether plain, carved or with painted decoration, are a useful item in several parts of the house. Near the garden entrance you can use one for rubbers, children's gum boots and playthings; by the fireplace you can store logs in one; and in the front hall it can form a receptacle for stormy weather kit or as a storage place for anything at all, while the top is handy for the temporary deposit of hats, gloves, and even outdoor garments. If it is not too low it can also act as a hall table. In none of these locations will the chest seem out of place.

In our old houses today we use more and more furniture pieces that are built in or made specially to fit some odd space. In these houses some interesting things can be done in adapting old furniture to modern fixtures. For example, an ancient and not-too-good commode, low cupboard, or even a washstand can be used to frame a bathroom wash basin. A pair of the cupboards flanking an old-style kitchen sink provide modern counter tops with an antique air. You can then connect the two cupboards by a pair of doors, patterned on the old ones, and have an enclosed sink with storage space below.

The built-in principle can be extended very successfully to the Welsh dresser. It is only necessary to copy the antique scrollwork and paneling. The finish can be in the natural wood or one of the old-time paint colors. If the dresser is of the Pennsylvania type it can just as well be decorated in the Dutch manner.

Another piece of modern furniture that is often built in is the radio, phonograph, or television set. Some period-furniture manufacturers have recognized the possibilities of incorporating such equipment in really handsome reproduction pieces. Consequently there are available breakfront bookcases, secretaries, commodes, credenzas, and similar large 18th century pieces with accommodations for electronic apparatus.

The makers of such sets have gone to great lengths to enclose their products in cabinets that follow period designs, including Queen Anne, Chippendale, Sheraton, French Provincial, Federal, and Early American styles. In planning the furnishing of a Colonial living room or library it is worth while to consider the placing of the television set at an early stage. Like the fireplace it will be a focal point, and cannot be relegated to any odd corner as the music-making apparatus so often can.

Things Hanging on Walls

Most of the furniture in any old-time house is below dado level. The wall expanse above that height is then broken only by doors and windows and fireplaces, leaving occasional patches of unadorned plaster, paneling, or papered wall. We get decoration into the upper wall area through window hangings, through candelabra, tin trays, and china vases on the fireplace mantel, and perhaps by stenciled cornices. The rest of the space offers a challenge to our decorating skill—and our taste.

It also provides an opportunity that few hesitate to take advantage of, though not always with happy results. Fortunately in the old-time house, we have reliable guides as to the kinds of decorative accessories we can tack onto our walls.

In the very early houses, and especially those with board or panel walls, considerable restraint is necessary. The woodwork itself usually has ample decorative value, especially when unpainted, and only an occasional accent is needed to relieve the monotony. But where there are expanses of plaster walls, papered or not, we can display with advantage our favorite pictures and other framed objects including mirrors and quill-work sconces, or even scraps of ancient wall hangings, and maybe a clock.

Of all these things mirrors and clocks have the advantage of being useful as well as ornamental. All we have to be sure of is that they are in keeping with the furniture style or period.

Mirrors are said to make rooms seem larger, but that is a general statement that needs qualifying. A mirror is like a window—it has the same effect as a source of daylight. Therefore hanging a large mirror is like making another opening in the wall. But the mirror must be where it can reflect light, and be looked into, otherwise it is no more effective in enlarging a room than a picture would be.

Small mirrors and looking glasses actually have little effect on the apparent room size at all, and in many rooms it takes a ceiling-high pier glass to produce any worthwhile effect of space. And so, in our old-time rooms we cannot rely much on mirrors for creating optical illusions.

Very few looking glasses large enough to hang on the wall existed in the colonies prior to the late 1600s, and most of those were in the larger Southern houses. In a great many homes there may have been a hand glass or two before 1700, but those do not enter into any discussion of decorating. By 1700, however, larger mirrors were being imported, though they were quite expensive. Most of them were narrow in proportion to their height, and the taller ones were made of two pieces of glass.

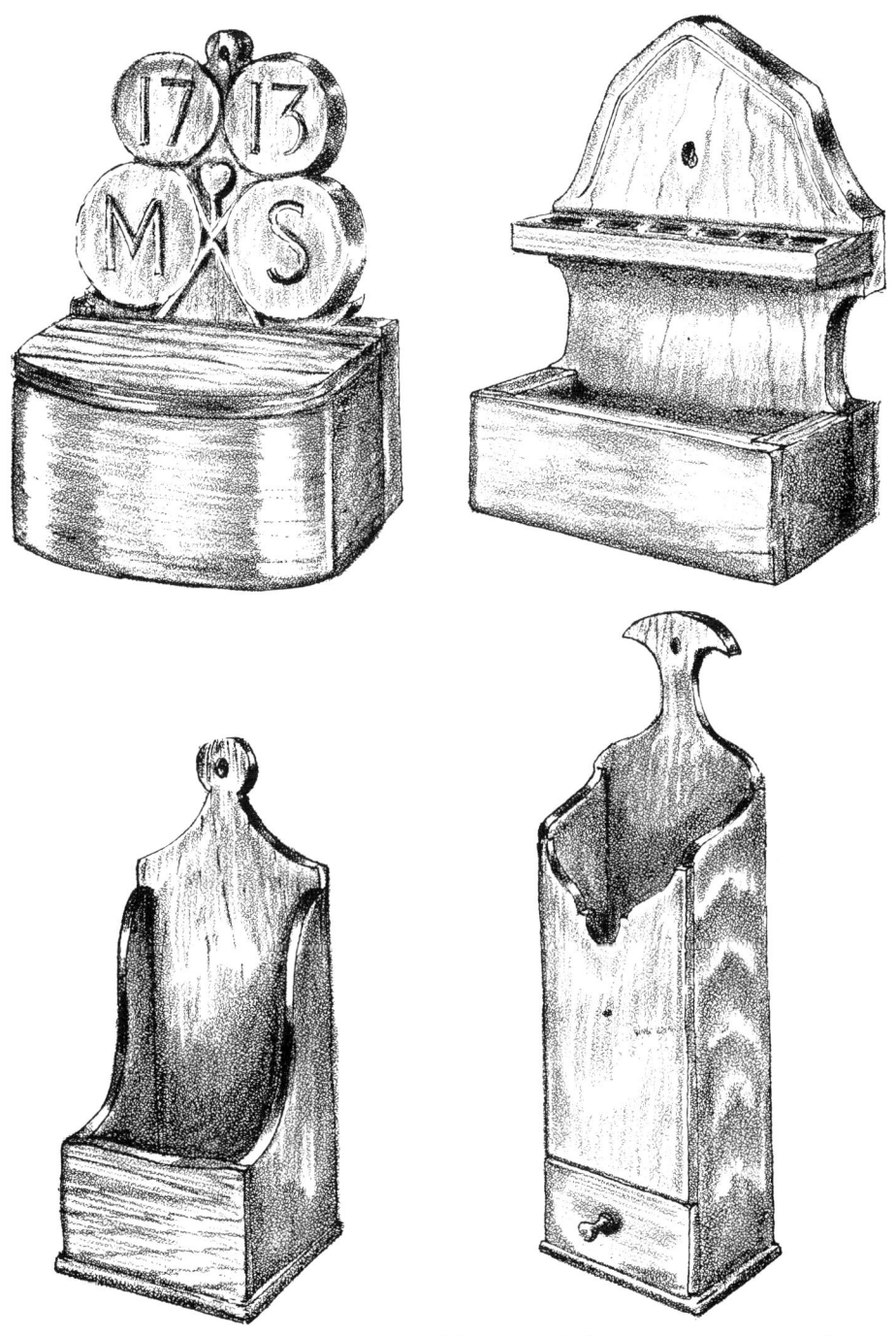

The addition of items like these old-timers helps to create atmosphere
in any Colonial room. They may be used on the wall or table.

Magnificent Sheraton sideboard for the formal dining room. The mirror is somewhat more elaborate than those seen in the average home.

Starting with the Queen Anne period style of glass we have a variety to choose from. The typical large, Queen Anne mirror, dated somewhat after Queen Anne's time, might be about 17 inches wide and a little over three feet tall, probably in a walnut veneered frame. The bottom part of the frame, containing the lower section of glass, would be rectangular in shape. The top piece of glass would be shaped to fit the Flemish scroll or cyma curves of the upper part of the frame. The frame molding might be anywhere from two to four inches wide, and many of them were japanned or gilded.

Somewhat similar looking glasses were made in large numbers between 1700 and 1720, and many of them had brass sconces or candle-holders attached. The frames, however, were so individual that it would be hard to ascribe them to any period at all. In making use of them today we would have to judge each glass according to its merits, using the simple ones in the more primitive rooms and the more highly finished and decorated specimens with the period furniture that suited them best.

A great many mirrors were brought from Venice, and those dated around 1740 are extremely ornate. Painted and gilded, they were ornamented with carvings of fruits and flowers, some topped by a scroll pediment, and bird finial! And these were real mirrors, some over six feet tall.

At the same time there were available small and simple looking glasses with pine and maple backs, some of them decorated with simple scrolls and jigsaw work. Less common, but of more interest to us today, were the highly decorated and carved little courting mirrors. The Chinese versions in particular, with their mirrored glass-inset frames and painted-picture crests add a touch of glamor to almost any 18th century walnut or mahogany room.

Sometime in the 1740s a long, low type of mirror became popular for mantel decoration. This type was often made up of three pieces of glass in a row, the joints being hidden by molding. At this time, the small dressing glasses also appeared. These were of various shapes—shield, round, square, oval, etc. and were held between vertical arms mounted on a drawer case.

Mirrors of the Early Georgian era were for the most part architectural in design. But in the pre-Chippendale era they began to be embellished with all sorts of decorative devices—medallions, shells, ribbons, and scroll-work of all kinds. Chippendale himself set the fashion for delicate gilt frames in lacy filigree of a distinctly oriental flavor. Other mirrors, usually called Chippendale, have perfectly flat frames of wood cut into fantastic outlines with a scroll saw. A common name for them is the silhouette mirror and they are very effective against a light background, as that name might

A fretwork mirror with beveled glass, of 1760 or so, which goes well with many Queen Anne and Chippendale pieces.

suggest. These silhouette mirrors, as it happens, do accord in feeling with Chippendale furniture.

Around 1790, Hepplewhite designed mirrors with a more classical touch, adorned with urns and swags atop the slender columnar frame side members. At about the same time Portuguese (Bilbao) mirrors were introduced. They had frames inset with thin marble strips, often salmon color.

Immediately after the Revolution mirror styles changed radically. The

This Queen Anne reproduction mirror, made in two pieces, has a lac-quered frame decorated in the Chinese manner.

country was soon inundated with a flood of so-called tabernacle mirrors. These are often quite wrongly called Sheraton mirrors. They are tall, rectangular glasses with pilastered sides and a decorated cornice. The upper third of the frame is occupied by a painting on glass, or a decorated and carved panel of gilded wood.

A contemporary of the tabernacle mirror was the girandole which even today has decorative possibilities in late 18th century rooms. Once quite fashionable, the girandole in its original form was a small mirror framed in gilt sprays of flowing lines and irregular shape. To the base was attached a pair of candle sockets. This type is reminiscent of the Chinese Chippendale

Two beautiful Chippendale style mirrors.

mirrors, but later the Federal influence substituted a circular convex mirror in a round gilt frame decorated with a ring of balls, richly carved top and bottom and surmounted by an eagle rampant. In rooms decorated in the Federal style or with Phyfe furniture they do not look amiss.

Other Framed Items

The very human craving for pretty things to look at found expression in the very early days of Colonial life. Those who could afford them had

Reproduction of a Chippendale rook mirror over a more somber chest.

tapestries; others had to be satisfied with the less decorative materials. Early in the 18th century fancy needlework was framed and hung up for admiration, and a little later quill-work became fashionable. Most quill-work samples appear to have been used as candle sconces in which role they were particularly effective. Otherwise they needed to be hung where the light would catch them.

Painting on glass also became a popular pastime for ladies of leisure. Teachers of this art were advertising as early as 1738. A great many of these paintings were provided with backgrounds of crumpled and colored tin foil which gave them the name of tinsel pictures. In the humbler homes parental pride, and no doubt an appreciation of primitive art, led to the display of daughter's sampler, fittingly framed. Such samplers were made in the 17th century and the practice was continued well into the 19th.

Toward the end of the 18th century pictorial needlework became the rage. Much of it was done with floss or twisted silk on canvas, satin, or silk, in a wide variety of colors.

In the earliest Colonial homes of any distinction we would find ancestral portraits done in oils, but no other kind of painting was available for many years to the middle class homes. For the first 150 years practically all of the painting done in this country was portraits. Not till late in the 18th century were genre paintings and landscapes produced. The first engravings were made around 1727, but little that was suitable for framing appeared before 1750. At that time also European prints were beginning to be imported, including engravings by Hogarth and others.

All of these are suitable for wall decoration in Colonial homes, provided some discrimination is used. Then there are many kinds of engravings and woodcuts, oil and water colors that were developed during the first part of the 19th century. Some of them look quite well and not at all out of place in Colonial rooms. The subject, however, is important, as is the coloring, if any, and the framing. All should conform to the styles current in the chosen period.

In recent years there has been an enthusiastic revival of interest in Currier and Ives prints. These were a product of the 1860s and many originals and reproductions have found their way into Colonial and Early American houses. Unfortunately these prints are neither Early American nor art. They are vastly interesting Americana; but they should not be framed nor should they be hung on walls in houses furnished in Colonial or Early American styles.

Old Timepieces

Both useful and decorative additions to any wall are the clocks of Colonial days. But the chronology of clock styles is apparently quite puzzling to those who are not collectors.

The earliest clocks used in the colonies were brought from England, Holland, France, and Sweden, but the records seem to show that the English clocks were the most numerous. These clocks, like most clocks of that time, were made entirely of brass. The most popular model for a long time was a wall clock incorporating an alarm. It was generally supported on a small shelf attached to a bed post.

This clock had but one hand—minutes were not so precious in those days—a domed top and sides of brass fretwork, and a pendulum; and over the years, has acquired a variety of names. It is known as the Cromwellian, birdcage, lantern clock, and so on, but none exists outside of collections.

About 1680 another kind of timepiece, miscalled a bracket clock, made its appearance here. It had a wooden case with a brass handle on top, and was supposed to stand on a table or mantel shelf. Then, as more people became able to own clocks, the famous wag-on-the-wall type gained favor. Of Dutch origin, it had a long exposed pendulum from which it gets its name.

The venerable grandfather, or tall-case, clock first appeared here in 1720, and the smaller edition, which we call the grandmother clock, was not made till after 1785. Most of the clocks mentioned so far had brass faces. The painted and enameled faces were not introduced till 1783.

Most of the old-time clocks with which we are familiar today were not made till after 1800. The deservedly popular banjo clock was invented by Simon Willard in 1802. This was followed by several models of shelf or mantel clocks, many of them in fancy cases of mahogany, cherry, or even oak. The more expensive ones were inlaid with satinwood or holly.

In 1812 Eli Terry made mantel clocks with scroll tops and decorated panels below the face, and standing on feet. French clocks were imported at about this time, many of them of exceedingly rich and fanciful design. Alabaster cases were common, often combined with gold faces and decorative side pillars, the whole being protected from dust by a glass bell or dome.

The Terry clocks are eminently suitable for the simpler types of house, and the French clocks go well with oriental rugs and furniture of the classic periods in furnishing and the Early Federal. For the pre-Georgian periods

English pendulum clock, made in 1665, with a short "bob" or pendulum. This model runs for twelve hours and strikes the hour.

The popularity of the banjo clock stems from its origin, about 1802. The first clock to hang on the wall, it ran for eight days.

*The mantel or shelf clock, made about 1808, had wooden works and ran
for thirty hours. This popular case has brass finials and painted door.*

Interesting example of a Colonial grandfather clock of about 1750 with case of cherry wood. Right, elaborate eight-day Dutch clock made in 1725.

*The "steeple" clock represents a model made by the thousands after 1837
when clocks with brass works were manufactured in quantity.*

we can use almost any of the less ornate clocks cased in pine, oak, maple, or
even walnut, or perhaps painted wood. The Georgian of course calls for
more decorative cases, preferably in mahogany with brass spandrels.

One of the most popular clocks today, possibly because they are still
easily obtainable, is the steeple clock, so-called because of the shape of its
peaked front and side spires. It is a mantel clock and has painted glass in
the lower section of the door. These were made in quantity about 1840.

ENGLISH FURNITURE PERIODS

DATES	PERIOD	
1485—1603	*Tudor and Elizabethan*	} "The Age of Oak"
1603—1689	*Jacobean and Restoration*	
1689—1702	*William-and-Mary*	"The Age of Walnut"
1702—1714	*Queen Anne*	(Dutch influence)
1714—1820	*Early Georgian & Georgian*	"Age of Mahogany and
1820—1830	*Empire*	Satinwood"

ENGLISH GEORGIAN FURNITURE DESIGNERS

1735—1779	*Thomas Chippendale*	Dutch, Gothic, Chinese, & French
1760—1786	*George Hepplewhite*	influence
1762—1792	*Robert Adam—architect*	Classical & French influence
1790—1806	*Thomas Sheraton*	

APPROXIMATE FURNITURE PERIODS IN AMERICA

1608—1720	*Early Colonial*—German, English, Dutch, Swedish influence in North; French & Spanish in South.	
1720—1780	*American Georgian*—English influence	
1780—1830	*Federal and Empire*—French influence	

NOTE: Pilgrim furniture was not a style or a period, but a term applied to early primitive pieces made in this country. Phyfe was a well-known maker of furniture, but his work is not classified as design.

II

TODAY

MODERN HOME—COLONIAL AIR: *Recreating the essence of an earlier age—The meaning of comfort and taste—Furniture grouping faults—Furnishing the Early American country house— A typical entry and living room.*

In the foregoing pages we have taken a brief excursion through the history of house furnishing in America. We have noted the kinds of furniture and furnishings used by our ancestors in the various periods and perhaps learned that while names are a guide to furniture styles what really matters is excellence of design and good workmanship regardless of whose name is tacked onto the piece. Some idea also has been gleaned of the combinations used in the various types of Old American houses during each period, and their possibilities for present-day use.

From all of this information we may now hope to plan rooms in Old American styles of houses that are suited to modern living, rooms that will create for us the modern backgrounds of Old American homes with the opportunities they offer for gracious living in an atmosphere of restful charm. In doing this we have to recognize that not all Old American houses formed the kinds of homes we would wish to duplicate today. Therefore we have to be selective and choose only those features that we judge will produce the desired effect with reproductions of old-time furniture and furnishings and modern adaptations of them. In other words we are not seeking to reproduce old homes so much as recapturing the spirit of the more charming homes of another and more gracious era, a spirit that was lost sometimes during the late Federal period and has not yet been rediscovered.

The time has now come for us to look into the possibilities of recreating the essence of this earlier age with things made today in the styles developed during Colonial days—the furniture, fabrics, wall and floor coverings and accessories.

149

In planning the furnishing of our Old American house we take it for granted that our primary objective will be to achieve comfort combined with good taste. But in order to do this we must first make sure that we understand what these terms imply. For example, the comfort that we speak of must surely refer to the comfort of all who use the rooms, and that includes visitors and children as well as the principal adults of the household. Furthermore, that comfort will have to consist of a great deal more than the mere provision of a sofa and cozy chair or two.

If a room is to be comfortable to stay in it must be satisfying in every way; there must be no distracting elements or ugly features. The furniture must be arranged so that each piece is properly accessible to one person without disturbing others. And when the seats are occupied they must not be subject to any annoyances such as poor lighting or facing too-bright windows.

The modern fetish of conversation groups is often carried to excess and easily becomes bad manners in furnishing. Except in the very largest rooms there is no necessity or excuse for crowding a sofa and a pair of chairs around a fireplace to the exclusion of everything—and everyone—else. A fire can be enjoyed without sitting on top of it, and anyone entering a room should not have to circumnavigate deliberate obstacles or face an overstuffed barricade in seeking any particular seat.

All this means is that a room should be inviting as a whole and not divided into fortified islands by exclusive groupings. This is one aspect of comfort that is too often overlooked or ignored. We want furniture arranged so that it can be moved around without spoiling patterns or groups. And we want rooms that appeal not merely to our critical faculties, but to our emotions as well.

Good taste involves a number of factors that it is as well to catalogue in advance. The first essentials, of course, are suitability and sincerity. Each piece of furniture should be chosen primarily for some specific purpose that it is designed for and which it can fill better than anything else. That much is obvious but it is equally important that the piece be suited to its surroundings. For example, you may find, and fall in love with, a perfectly adorable 18th century commode. You can think of nothing that would be more useful in your entrance hall, serving both as a table and giving you much needed storage space. You quite overlook, or brush aside, the fact that it is far too pretentious a piece for your style of house or the rest of your furniture. When once you see it in place you realize (we hope) that though it serves a purpose it is not suitable, and if you are wise you will quickly substitute a simple old chest instead.

Sincerity in furniture as in people is lack of pretense. Insincerity is often manifested in overornamentation, but it is also revealed in an effort to achieve an atmosphere of antiquity through the display of useless and unbeautiful relics of a more primitive age. The truth is that sincerity can only be achieved through the character of the room as a whole. It must be "built-in"—it cannot be tacked on as an afterthought.

Probably the most elusive quality of all is what we call charm. Charm is not something that we can deliberately plan for, but the astounding thing is that if we plan right, and do not go seeking after effects, we shall capture it just the same. Of course there are different degrees and flavors of charm, and its quality will differ with the kind of house and what goes in it.

An air of comfort is the first step toward charm but it must be comfort that is obviously well cared for, and you cannot have that in a shabby room. Shabbiness, luckily, can be avoided even with old things by having good ones in the first place. Good old things will seem beautiful because of the quality that shines through; like genuinely good people they grow old gracefully. Being well-worn just gives the furniture pieces an air of having long belonged where they are. They look settled, and that is another basic requirement of charm—an air of rightness. A pristine, newly furnished room is likely to be lacking in that respect. But do not make the mistake of thinking that everything very old is nice. If it was not attractive when it was first made it never will be in a thousand years. The ideal home then is filled with old things lovingly cared for, and new ones that are chosen with care.

Another important ingredient is an air of hospitality. Some homes and some rooms seem to invite you to enter. They are the cheerful, unpretentious kind, but that does not mean that they are without dignity. Like a particular person they can be friendly without abandoning all reserve. It is that reserve and dignity that calls forth our respect.

These, then, are the things we should aim for in our furnishing. We are not simply furnishing a set of rooms; we are making a home. And through our choice of an Old American house, and the furniture that tradition dictates must go with it, we are seeking to capture that extra something that modern houses and modern furnishing cannot give us—a sense of permanence and continuity. If we are successful we shall have a home that our friends will love to enter; a home that is attractive and restful, harmonious and well-cared-for, regardless of the degree of formality that our personality and position demand; a home where we can escape from turmoil into serenity by the mere lifting of a latch.

And so with these ideals and principles in mind let us see how our Old

American home can be furnished to our lasting satisfaction through the choice of furniture and furnishings that will suit both ourselves and the kind of house we live in.

The Small Early American

If yours is a country house of the Early American, central-chimney style, your furnishing skill will be sharply challenged the moment you open the front door. Here you will find yourself in an entry, perhaps only seven feet wide and half as deep, from which a stair climbs abruptly to the second floor.

Obviously there is no room for furniture here, and the most you can do is something clever with wall treatment and rug, and perhaps a lighting sconce. Color will be your most useful tool.

Your choice of furniture period will, of course, be largely a matter of personal preference. But if your inclinations are toward the thoroughly informal, the unsophisticated farmhouse type, with early maple ladderback chairs, and so on—the Early American Provincial would be most suitable. It would be a wise choice because it gives you great latitude in your selection of pieces, background patterns and colors. The furniture can include any piece of Colonial furniture that the owner of such a house would be likely to possess in Colonial times—that is, furniture of the quality and style he would be likely to afford and have a taste for. Stated plainly, it should not be too grand for the house nor so crude as to reflect on the owner's taste.

In this small house, then, the staircase may be painted in any one of a variety of old-time colors. You might, for instance, use cream or ivory for all woodwork including the stair risers, but the stair treads would be chocolate brown or dark green at least in the center. If you find this a little too drab and ordinary, you can paint all the woodwork Indian red or one of the early blue-grays. The red however is rarely suitable in such large doses except for the most primitive dwellings. It is a lovely color to use for accents and has a real old-time flavor. If the house happens to have unplastered ceilings and lots of raw woodwork you might be justified in stripping off all the paint and using the natural wood. But you would have to be sure the woodwork at present under the paint was good and therefore originally intended to be left exposed.

In the entry you might have a door to the cupboard under the stairs. If this has old hinges do not make the mistake of painting them black. That is a modern conceit that spoils the authentic air of many a house.

A stair landing provides room for a charming little retreat. Early birds-eye maple desk, painted chest, and Sheraton "fancy" chair.

The floor of your entry is probably of wide boards of pine or oak, running parallel with the front wall. Nicely oiled or waxed boards need no other covering. But if you must have a mat let it be one that is easily cleaned and not readily damaged. Light-colored hooked rugs are out of place here for both these reasons. A small braided rug will do if the colors go well with your paint work. A good alternative would be a simple rag rug, or a strip of cotton or linen woven rug such as you might use for a stair runner.

More often than not the stairs would be left bare, but for quietness' sake you might prefer to cover the treads with a simple linen woven runner of a solid color. That color should approximate one of the old-time tones listed earlier in this volume.

In case you do use a runner, you have to consider that there are (probably) two right angle turns in the stairs which make it difficult to fit the runner well without cutting it into three lengths. The runner should be tacked down in an inconspicuous manner; stair rods should not be used.

On the upper landing you again have a choice of bare wood floors or using a woven rug of tweedy character that suggests homespun. The wood finish should be the same as that of the entry and stairs.

The plain plaster of the ceiling and stair wall obviously cries for some decoration, but to maintain the simple air you cannot use anything that is not utilitarian as well as decorative. And what you use must not occupy traffic space. One or a pair of simple lighting sconces can sometimes be used, either on the entry wall or at the foot of the stairs. In the latter position you may also (or instead) use a simple, small, old looking glass in a pine or maple frame, or painted some old-time color such as dark green or brown.

On the entry wall, a short peg-board can be nailed to hold raincoats, etc. Sometimes the stair layout permits the bottom step to be extended alongside the stair cupboard for a foot or two. You might be able to make that part of the step into a box by cutting through the tread and adding hinges so that it forms a lid. That would provide storage for rubbers. In other cases one of the panels of the stair closet can be made into a small cupboard, or even into a drawer for a similar purpose. This is occasionally done when the door to the closet is in the living room.

On the upstairs landing, you have a better chance for furnishing by standing a small chest or other narrow piece against the front wall—but don't use anything with drawers in it. The traffic here is more casual, but such a piece may be a serious obstruction in case of fire or other emergency. It is best left out entirely if the space is very narrow.

In the larger Early American house, or one with a more imposing entry, you can logically be a trifle more formal. For one thing you can decorate the entry and stairs with wallpaper, use a larger mirror, and perhaps install a useful piece of furniture or even a standing clock.

The paint work should be one of the standard old colors, but the plaster may be tinted. The wallpaper might use the paint color as the color of its pattern, but paint and background colors ordinarily should not be the same. The pattern of the wallpaper could be a medallion or other small figure, widely spaced and preferably on a light background so as to add to the apparent size of the entry. A strong pattern is usually a poor choice on these small and irregular wall areas.

If the stair proportions are such that the wallpaper carried to the second floor ceiling seems to heighten and shorten the entry, the pattern can be interrupted at the top of the stairs. This may be done by using a wallpaper border on the stair wall at the second floor level, or running a painted trim board across at that point. This breaks the vertical expanse in two. If necessary you can also use a somewhat darker paper above this dividing line, the landing often being lighter than the hall because of a central upstairs window.

Almost equally as effective as the wallpaper—and much more so than some—is a simple leaf stencil border on the stair and entry walls. This can be in greens or browns, perhaps with an occasional spot of red or yellow. The stencil may follow the ceiling line around both the entry walls and stair walls. It does not necessarily have to go to the second floor ceiling, and vertical lengths should be avoided because they give the walls a chopped up appearance in this confined space.

Another change you can make in the larger entry is to use a rag or braided rug. You can also use a stair runner of the same kind. A small table is always a convenience near the front door, but you cannot properly use a space-saving console type here. There are, however, simple gateleg tables with very narrow tops that can be fitted in.

Unless the entry is at least four and a half feet wide it is not advisable to use a tall clock here; a smaller one on a bracket is much more suitable. Under it can be placed some simple receptacle for umbrellas, parasols, and walking sticks. You can also use a larger mirror providing it has a simple frame. If you can find a very narrow old chest, or have one made for this location you will have a useful surface for hats, gloves, purses, etc. over which to hang the mirror, and storage space for things not often used, such as extra blankets, or picnic rugs. But nothing should project more than twelve or fifteen inches from the wall. In any entry less than five feet deep it is not advisable to place a chair there even if the front door will open wide without striking it.

In many of the smaller entries and some larger ones, the woodwork included a short seat running from the newel post alongside the stair closet. Such a fixture would therefore be quite in order today. This type of built-in seat takes up little room and serves also as a depository for trifles and as a storage box.

The Living Room

In the vast majority of really old colonial houses the kitchen has long ago become the living room. It contains a medium to large fireplace with extensive areas of wood around it, and is therefore the dominant feature of the room. There are two ways of incorporating this feature into the furnishing scheme. One is to play up the fireplace wall as the main center of interest; the other is to minimize it as much as possible by emphasizing some other feature.

The fireplace is of course the natural focal point in cold weather when the fire is lit. At other times it loses interest. But in these Early American houses where the rooms are small we cannot always turn our backs on the hearth. Because of a plethora of doors and windows we cannot do much shifting around of furniture anyway. In such cases the best that we can do is to add a secondary interest to the fireplace wall.

One successful way of doing this is to create a bright spot alongside the hearth with books. For some obscure reason, books do not seem to modernize a room so much as some other forms of decoration, especially if the bindings or jackets are subdued in tone and not violently modern in design. The bookcase idea is generally practical provided you have the books, because many of the Early American kitchen fireplaces had closets alongside them. This closet either went under, or at the side of, a stair to the upper floor. Quite often it is possible to switch that closet door into the entry and fill the old door frame with book shelves.

In place of the book shelves you may be able to build in a small china cabinet, preferably unpainted. This should be similar in appearance to the old built-in corner cupboards rejoicing in the old-time name of beaufatt, boffitt, etc., according to the spelling ability of the original owner. In the absence of either the books or a china or pewter display, some such piece of furniture as a small lamp table, or a pair flanking the fireplace can be used.

Where there is a bake oven, it is best covered with a batten door or even a more formal paneled door, and hidden from sight. Then a piece of

Unusually fine example of an 18th Century living room. Note corner cupboard, four-section ladder-back settle, needlework draperies, Pennsylvania library table, and roundabout chairs.

furniture can be placed against it. This procedure is almost essential when you have a chair or love seat on either side of the hearth.

If the fireplace is in a corner, as often happens, there is some difficulty in getting seats anywhere near the hearth on one side. The modern scheme of putting one love seat end-on to the fireplace does not work here. The best you can do is to use an early type of wing chair at the free side of the hearth. In some cases you can balance it with a pine settle against the wall. But to add to our difficulties, in this type of house, there is often a door in the wall against, and at right angles to, the fireplace.

Unless you can eliminate this door, or remove the entire wall, you cannot group seats around or near the fireplace. Occasionally the door can be moved farther from the hearth, but even then any seat placed in the corner is too near the fire for comfort.

Another problem in furniture placing is sometimes introduced by the presence of a funeral door in the wall facing the fireplace. Luckily this door can be more or less ignored because it rarely needs to be opened. It can be straddled by a sofa or perhaps hidden behind a highboy, a screen, or a hanging shelf most of the time.

The normal Early American front kitchen, used as a living room, will have four doors, three of which cannot be ignored. It will also perhaps have two windows if it is in its original state, or three if it has been modernized. There is therefore little clear wall space except that facing the front windows. The small room still may be able to accommodate a sofa, tavern table, a pair of candle stands used as end tables, a joint-stool coffee table, a wing chair, two or three side chairs, a nest of occasional tables, and perhaps a small slant-top desk which might serve as a resting place for the telephone. Above the tavern table you might have a wall cabinet, or the low desk can be replaced with a secretary. But in such a small room any tall piece of furniture should not project far from the wall, and anything hung on the wall should be flat, and light in feeling. Pictures and mirrors are ideal, as is a shelf no more than seven inches deep and fairly light in appearance though solid in construction. You will get a better feeling of space if you restrict your furniture pieces to a height not much above the dado. If you need bookcases perhaps you can use a Welsh dresser which can be wide without looking too topheavy.

For the simplest of Early American rooms some of the Pilgrim style pieces or the later American Provincial will give an air of cozy informality. The principle to be followed here, however, is to choose pieces that are really timeless as far as period is concerned. For instance, the very early

The other end of the 18th Century living room on page 157, showing its handsome panelled fireplace wall with pilasters and raised panels. The chandelier is unusual and interesting, as is the day bed.

little butterfly table has been so much used and copied in so many sizes and variations that it seems to belong in almost any unsophisticated room. Other pieces could be pine, cherry, maple, or oak tavern tables of any vintage, a rush-seated roundabout chair to go with the pine slant-top desk, slat-back chairs or the more dignified, and earlier, banister backs, or even Windsors.

If the room is fairly large you may find a corner for a small cupboard. Among the more modern pieces you would probably want an upholstered love seat. On the other hand if you are considering a full-sized sofa it is as well to remember that they often take up more space than they justify. The ordinary three-cushion sofa is not particularly comfortable for three people; the unfortunate individual in the middle cannot properly relax and may even acquire a stiff neck turning to one side and the other conversing with his neighbors. The only time the extra length is justified is in using the sofa as a day bed. This is worth thinking of in furnishing any small room.

Apart from this a great many Early American rooms do include successfully such tributes to modern comfort as a small-scale Lawson, Tuxedo, or Queen Anne sofa, a barrel chair or a Martha Washington arm chair. But in each case the piece should be covered with a suitable fabric. Incidentally, cottons became the rage in the early 1700s, and chintzes and India prints were used in all classes of homes throughout the colonies. As a rule, however, for the early informal rooms sofas and chairs are best covered in an all-over patterned chintz or one of the newer stencil-pattern calico prints, or even a cotton rep in solid color, perhaps with a ruffle of the same material.

Wall and Floor Finishes

To maintain an air of simple informality the plaster walls should be an off-white and the wood painted ivory or cream or a blue-gray, or else left natural. For a little more formal touch you can add a pale tint to the plaster or use a stencil border in color, but any plaster ceiling should be left white. The mottled ceilings and woodwork that you sometimes see belong to a much later period.

If you have the original floor in wide oak or pine they are best left in their natural state, and oiling is generally better than waxing, provided it is properly done. If the floors have narrow boards and are not too good you will probably get much better effect by painting them all over. It would also be in order to apply a stenciled border or panel, as previously described, or relieve the bareness with an occasional stenciled figure such as a leaf or a geometric design. This decorating would date the house toward the 19th century but, using the proper colors, you can get an effect no more modern than that of the earliest painted canvas floor coverings. And whatever you did would be an improvement on the modern flooring.

For furnishing in the very earliest period, or for almost any period at all, you can hardly improve on the bare floors if they are good. On the other hand, housekeeping is somewhat simplified if you have a small rug or two to throw down where there is most traffic, or in front of seats and under tables. Here you have a useful choice of color, design and texture in braided rugs, woven cotton or linen ones in an overall color, or the later hooked rugs of an informal and somewhat primitive design. The geometric or tile-effect hooked rugs are particularly adapted for use in the larger sizes.

Window Treatments

The windows in the average living room in the small Early American house are best treated simply, with no shades of any kind. The ruffled organdy or dotted Swiss curtains, perhaps tied back but with absolutely no crossover, give a simple cottage effect that is charming with provincial furniture.

Much of the effect you secure with both curtains and draperies will be due in no small measure to the way the curtains are cut and hung. This is so important a feature of the Early American room, and one that is so often neglected to its detriment, that it may be as well to devote a little space to a discussion of authentic curtain arrangements and modern interpretations of them.

In the first place the early curtains were hung on poles or rods of wood, generally of small diameter. The curtains were suspended from this rod by loops of the same material, from half an inch to an inch wide depending on the weight of the curtain. With this arrangement the curtains could easily be drawn across the windows at night and be used at other times to help keep out the cold.

The curtains were made sill length which means that they ended short of the actual sill or ledge of the window frame. Generally the pole was set into the window aperture (the reveal) and not fastened to the outer edge of the window stile as is the custom today.

Another pleasing curtain arrangement was that called the Dutch or "country" style of hanging. This involved making the curtain in two sections—one for the upper half of the window and the other for the lower half. Each would be on its own rod and made of some sheer material. Here again the entire window frame was left exposed, both rods being set within

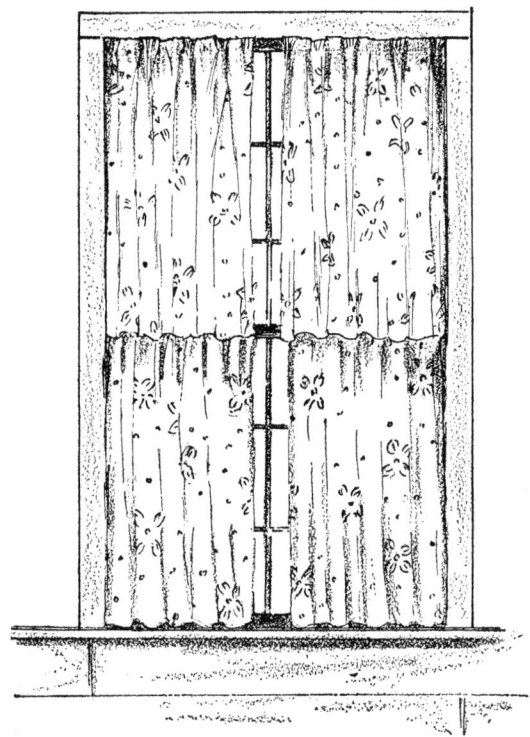

*Proper length for curtains in the Early American house is to sill, with
fixture brackets set inside the frame of the window.*

it. In this case, instead of loops of material it is generally better to use plastic
or brass rings. They slide more easily on the rod and make prettier folds in
the curtains when they are drawn back.

Since most of us are lovers of light and sunshine, in these days we
would probably prefer to raise the upper section of the curtains to the top
of the window lintel, suspending the curtains from there. It is a good idea
to do this when only a ruffle is used in place of the upper curtain.

If the two sections of curtain are of unequal length you can still maintain pleasing proportions between them by using a little artifice. For instance if your small-paned windows are "twelve-over-nines" the bottom
curtain section will be shorter than the upper one when you mount the lower
rod at meeting rail height. You can equalize the appearance if you use a
ruffle over the top section and apply a band decoration to the bottom of the
lower one.

There are almost endless decorating possibilities with this country style

The "double," "Dutch," or country type curtain may be hung on a window where the number of lights in the two sashes is unequal. Use of a top ruffle (right) helps to widen the tall, narrow window.

of window dressing. But in all cases if you do not need the protection of shades it is as well to entirely eliminate them because of the bulky roller. You could always use a simple glass curtain close against the window and hang over it the two-sectioned curtains which could be drawn for privacy. In this case a heavier material of solid color could be used for the draw-curtains, or a gay figured chintz, or calico with a solid-color background, edged with a ruffle or ball-fringe, or colored tape.

In a room furnished with Pennsylvania Dutch furniture the curtains could well be of muslin with a peasant-design border down the inner long edge and across the bottom. On the other hand if your room is furnished principally with French Provincial pieces you have an opportunity of using the bright warm yellows, and reds and vivid greens in solid masses, or in stripes.

Among the earlier materials used for these window-length draperies (they should never extend below the sill in these early houses) are: calicoes, printed linens and cottons, homespuns, India prints, and chintzes—all of which can be obtained in reproduction designs today.

The Accessories

For the Early American living room the lighting equipment needs to be subdued rather than emphasized. Floor lamps are of the bridge type made of black iron, or replicas of the old wooden candle stands. In both cases the shades should be simple conical ones of plain parchment or cloth. Preferably they should be natural or of a solid color that will blend in well with the colors of the rugs and upholstery. Table and reading lamps with a delightfully unsophisticated air can be evolved from old glass or pewter whale-oil lamps, old wooden mortars, earthenware jugs, pewter tankards, or copper vessels of various kinds—all objects found in these old rooms in their original unglorified state.

Of course you can't properly use overhead lights unless they are of the lantern type or replicas of primitive chandeliers described earlier, neither of which is suited to a living room. Wall sconces of the early type however can be used effectively, but they should be reserved for rooms where a little formality is desired.

Fireplace equipment should be of black iron, but polished steel does not look out of place.

On the walls of even the small houses oil portraits are effective and authentic, but little damage is done if we also use simple pastorals or genre paintings that are mellow and subdued. The only other type of framed decoration should be samplers and small unadorned mirrors. Decorative accents however can be provided by hanging small wall boxes, either in plain pine or painted, such as pipe boxes, key cupboards, etc. at strategic points.

Of all the available clocks—the earliest types being such rarities—the banjo style and the pillar-and-scroll, and steeple mantel clocks seem most at home in these early surroundings.

I2

OTHER EARLY COLONIAL ROOMS: *Combining room func-tions—Furnishing the dining room—Bedroom pieces and back-grounds—Early Colonial kitchens—French Provincial pieces.*

In the little houses with lots of rooms, room functions do not need to be combined. Each room can serve one special purpose without multiplying housekeeping problems. Our observation is that you can indulge in much more gracious living if you have separate living and dining rooms, and per-haps separate dens or studies or play rooms for those members of the family who need them. Quite often, it seems, the craze for oversize rooms is carried to excess and is not always supported by reason. The urge seems to stem largely from families used to living in cramped apartments who, in their enthusiasm on moving to a house, go to the other extreme. Knocking out walls in these Early American houses actually is something that needs to be considered seriously and long before going ahead. Light and air are not the only things you expect of a house, old or new.

If you have a Northern style Early American house which has not been rearranged internally you will probably be able to use the long room behind the chimney as a dining room. To be sure, it will be narrow, but with extra windows, or one big one with small panes and deeply recessed, and a table made to measure, you will not find it too small for the average-sized family. Nine out of ten of these old houses which have originally had three ground-floor rooms at the rear will today have but two. Either the old borning room or the old pantry will have been added to what was the second kitchen. In the old saltboxes especially an ell was added and the house rooms re-arranged to conform. The result is usually a longer but of course no wider room.

If you cannot find an old trestle table not more than twenty inches

Early American dining room with the original floor, in poor condition, covered with a tile composition simulating random width boards. The trestle table is a reproduction; chairs and cupboard are originals.

wide you can always have one made from a couple of old pine boards. One eminently suitable old trestle table has a top only 18 inches wide, but there is a hinged leaf along each side six inches wide. The table then can be made 18, 24, or 30 inches wide, according to the needs of the moment. With this type of table nothing goes so well, or takes up so little room as simple, rush-seated ladder-back or spindle-back chairs. An alternative would be an early refectory type of table with stretchers. This of course would call for a more solid style of chair such as the Carver type or the heavier turned chairs with plain feet. As a general rule, though, heavy furniture does nothing for a small room except make it seem crowded.

Much more to be preferred are the narrower folding tables such as an oblong or narrow oval gateleg, a trestle gateleg, or even a butterfly table which can be pushed aside when not in use. Either the drawer type of table or one with two end leaves is good because each enables you to regulate the size according to your requirements.

Several styles of chair go well with the Jacobean gatelegs, particularly the turned New England chairs with slat backs, though some banister-backs and early cane-back chairs with Spanish or scroll feet are in keeping. But always the more open the backs the lighter and less bulky will the chairs appear and therefore more suited to the small room.

With tables of lighter construction, either bow-back or fan-back Windsor chairs are ideal. Furthermore they can be had in a variety of natural woods or painted. Painted Windsors of the dining room types are not common nowadays, but in the early times they were plentiful. The same may be said of the early banister-back chairs, especially those dating back to 1725 or earlier. Their beautiful semi-transparent finishes in reds, greens, and black did not entirely kill the texture of the wood (as does the opaque coating of modern paint), and can be copied with profit today. These colored chairs look very well with pine, maple or cherry tables and other dining room pieces in the natural wood. They give the room a distinctive flavor that is pleasing as well as different, and quite authentic.

Other fascinating combinations are braced bow-back Windsors with a pine hutch table, and bamboo-turned Windsors with a plain turned gateleg table. Even the large drop-leaf table so popular today—most of them date from around 1810 or later—can be made to seem very much at home in the early dining room. The favorites seem to be of cherry, but they have quite an air when surrounded by painted and decorated "fancy" chairs of the Hitchcock type, or even the humbler arrow-backs of around the same vintage. In the long room you may be able to put a painted cabinet or dresser

Modern interpretation of an 18th Century china cabinet.

Reproduction maple cabinet for use in hall, dining room or living room.

An informal dining room furnished with reproductions of Early American pieces, Windsor chairs and hooked rug. The window and wall treatment seen here is not representative of the true Early American room.

Another 20th Century dining room in Early American garb—this time with ladder-back chairs, hooked rug and patterned drapery fabric. Solid color draperies might have blended better with wallpaper and rug.

of the early New York Dutch or Pennsylvania types without having it seem over-dressed.

Most of these rooms have a small fireplace and a window or windows opposite, and sometimes three or four doors unevenly distributed. The salt-boxes are more likely to have a really large kitchen fireplace, and a door as well as windows facing it. In these instances the room will probably be deep enough to permit of adequate furnishing without a specially narrow table. Here you can probably use a Welsh dresser at one end, or a water bench as a side table. A corner cupboard may dress up the room besides holding the china and glassware. But you will probably find that one or a pair of small tables such as candlestands on the fireplace wall will perform surprisingly well as serving tables. Of course if there is ample room you can use a small chair-table or hutch table instead.

If the house is a very early saltbox with plenty of pine paneling you may have shallow cupboards flanking the fireplace. These are made even more decorative by removing the doors and filling them with book shelves. The dining room then can do double duty as a study room for which the long table is a great convenience.

In houses where the dining room is more square or more space has been acquired through the elimination of a wall, you have a great deal more scope in the pieces you can use and the formality you can achieve. You can begin to mix a little Queen Anne with your Jacobean, keeping the walnut banister-back chairs but banishing the cruder ladder-backs and Carvers. But, if you want comfort, never go quaint and use spindle back settees or benches of any kind for your guests at table, although they are quite authentic and add more than they take away from the early atmosphere.

And they do have advantages. The benches in particular take up little room in use and can be pushed out of the way under the table when the meal is over. But they are never comfortable when occupied by several people. No two persons feel at ease the same exact distance from the table, and the inability to make the slightest adjustment can be exasperating. If it happens that you have inherited a pair of these old forms or settees and feel bound to use them, the least you can do is to provide each guest with a separate seat cushion. As far as your own family is concerned this is, of course, a matter for your conscience.

If you happen to have a cell-like dining room with a predominance of white plastered walls you have a perfect background for the sober simplicity of Shaker furniture. This furniture is made in pine, walnut, beech, and maple, all of which are happy with trim that is painted blue-gray. The table

Excellent reproduction of a Pennsylvania type dresser with scalloped cornice and raised-panel doors. Adds interest to any dining room.

will probably be a long, foursquare trestle type, and if you have a Spartan temperament, as noted above, you can use a Shaker backed bench on either side of it. Otherwise, small straight-legged side chairs can be substituted. The remaining pieces of furniture might include: a plain sideboard; a tall, narrow, flat-fronted cupboard; a geometrically rigid set of wall shelves for pewter, etc.; a charming six-drawer chest three drawers high; with nothing but a table-sized woven rag rug on the floor. The very simplicity of such a room is striking and should not be spoiled by the use of overdecorated materials at the windows or luxurious accessories of any kind, primitive oil portraits excepted.

The Walls

With a dining room that has boarded or paneled walls your main decorating problem is settled for you. Natural pine to the ceiling makes a marvelous background for the table and its appointments, especially by candle-light or firelight. After dark the room seems to close in upon you, in a friendly way. It is not an oppressive sort of enfolding. Shadows and the warmth of old wood, with here and there a gleam of battered copper and old glass, create more of a protective aura that is comforting and satisfying and exudes antiquity.

Where there is no wood above the dado the plaster walls should be off-white, but here is a good place to give the room a certain warmth and coziness through the use of wallpaper that has the effect of a light pattern on a darker background. Some of the diamond-figured papers in tans and reds are particularly effective in tying together the wood surfaces of furniture and trim. The white wall of course silhouettes and separates them, and breaks the wall up into small patches.

Among the many alternatives you have for the dining room walls are painted trim and other woodwork in any of the old colors; tinted walls and darker painted dado, or stenciled walls on either white or some well-chosen ground color. If you paint the woodwork, the room should be furnished in a slightly more formal style than the primitive. Then you can paint all the trim and use a wallpaper with a background the same color as the paint. This again will tie the room together. On the other hand, if you have a long room, in proportion to the width, you can diminish the attenuated effect by stenciling the end walls only. The best effect is generally secured by stenciling in a light color on a dark background. But don't forget the warnings on color combinations contained in Book One.

In place of stenciling you can now get a variety of interesting and authentic stenciled wallpapers that reproduce the old effect perfectly. In the good papers the background has the effect of early plaster regardless of its color. To go with pine, maple, or even cherry, there is a rich green paper with widely separated stenciled figures in brown and white that is excellent, and green is a restful color. But do not make the mistake of using it in all the adjoining rooms as well, or even on stairs that are visible from the dining room. You can easily have too much of this good thing. Bold stencil patterns crawling like snakes all over the walls are apt to induce a restless feeling.

A much warmer background than the above is provided by a small diamond-pattern paper in white on deep red, but this calls for wood that is not too light in tone. Woodwork with a lot of yellow in it loses character against this background. One place in which you should not use the room wallpaper is in the backs of bookcases, or shelves for the display of china or metalware. A solid color such as an old gray-blue or even Indian red is usually much more effective and pleasing.

If you have walls of white plaster you have to rely principally on your draperies for color, but you can put colorful loose cushions on your chair seats, and use chair-back pads also if the chair style permits. The draperies and curtains should follow the rules outlined in connection with living rooms as to size, type, and placement. If you have plain wood walls you get a rich effect by using stencil pattern draperies over white glass or draw curtains. A yellow background with the design in dark green and red gives a sunny touch to the old wood-lined room.

Equally as effective as the stencil patterns are some modern adaptations of early cotton prints. The type is exemplified by a well-known pattern of stars and flowers in a black shaded design on a rich brown field. Others that seem to have a more cottagey effect are tiny spidery diaper-pattern calico prints, with bright red flowers and white dots on either a pale cocoa or a mustard yellow background. The same pattern has a striking effect with the flowers in blue or tile red—more colorful than a Southern mammy's dazzling bandana!

Under Foot

On a dining room floor bare old wood is the best decoration. But if you have a floor that needs a rug, use a rag rug of some type and stand the table on it. The rug can pick up one of the colors of the wall stencil or draperies. A mottled effect here usually seems more old and primitive than a solid-color rug, and does not so definitely create the effect of an island in the middle of the floor. Subdued colors are best for that reason. If it is a braided rug that you use this means that the outer rings of color should not contrast too strongly with the color of the floor.

When the floor is in poor condition and it is not practical to lay a new one, several problems may be solved by adding a new surface. One of the happiest solutions to the problem of a worn and cold floor with shrunken boards and open seams is a cork surface. Cork tile is available in a variety of shades of brown and in fairly large pieces. This enables you to lay a simulated wide board floor that is warm and air-tight, and quiet to walk on.

For rooms of a later period you might hide a shabby floor under paint that has been spatter-dashed. For a fairly large dining room the spattering can be confined to a rug-sized area by painting around it a simple line border. This is useful on any painted floor where there is much traffic, and particularly under a table. But the idea should be used with discretion. The moment you get runners or lanes of spattering you create the effect of a modern linoleum and destroy the antique feeling.

Illumination

In such a room as this old-time dining room, nothing can replace candlelight for the evening table. But you will need other lights besides those on the board. Over the table center you can have a wood-and-tin, brass, or pewter chandelier of a simple type for any number of candles. Authentic types which you can use in the electrified form were described earlier. For later rooms, the hanging whale-oil lamps or a double student-lamp type of hanging lamp can be used.

Over the fireplace, by the windows, or flanking bookcases and closets, you can have almost any number of wall sconces. For the more primitive room these should be of the shelf type; in later rooms the branch style in brass or bronze, is more in keeping.

In the earliest rooms the decorative accessories might well include a hanging clock that has a large dial and no case; wooden spoon and pipe racks, candle boxes of tin or wood, and plenty of pewter ware. Other wall decorations follow the schemes noted for Early American living rooms.

Early American Bedrooms

The dominating piece of furniture in any bedroom is of course the bed. In the little Early American house the bed therefore sets the pattern for the rest of the room.

Few people, and particularly women, can resist the appeal of a canopied bed, and consciously male members of the household who are inclined to decry such lace-hung fripperies as tester tops should remember that even George Washington slept under a canopy of crewel work and figured linen. This type of bed fortunately is both old and adaptable to informal and formal rooms.

In selecting a bed the choice is practically limited to tall-post or short-post beds. The highly popular spool bed is a 19th century creation that should be preserved for later houses. In the tall-post class there are several varieties of canopy beds but not all of them can be used in the small house because of the limited ceiling height.

For these houses the small arched tester bed called a field bed is deservedly popular. These beds have all the canopy that is desirable according to our modern notions, and they do not overpower the small room with

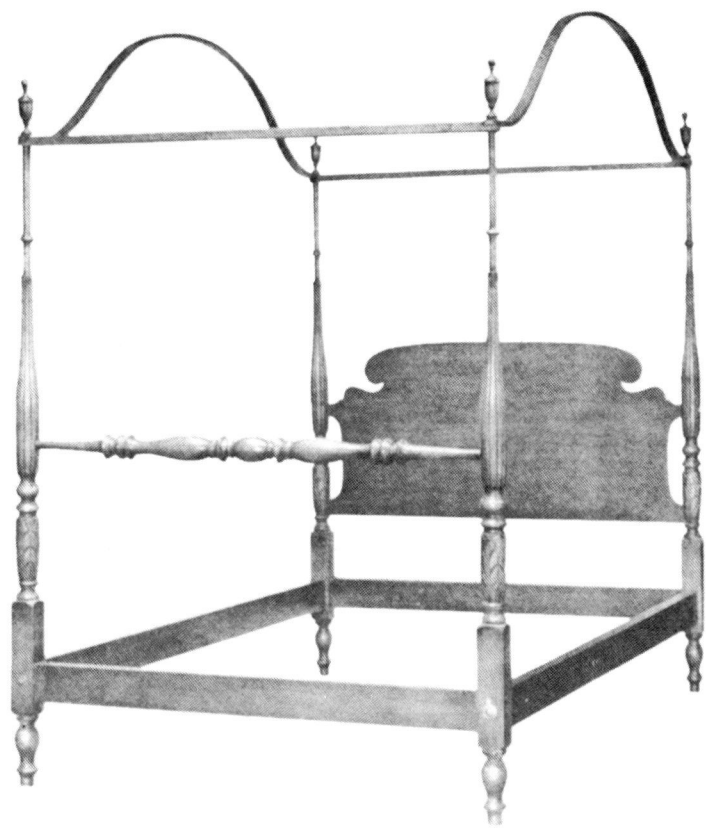

Skeleton of a canopy bed. The location of the blanket rail indicates the height of thick mattresses and feather bed used in its day.

masses of billowing draperies and hangings. The testers, too, can be of woven fabric or a lacy type to meet masculine or feminine requirements.

If the question of twin beds should arise it is best to forget the field bed. The striving for effect is too obvious in a small bedroom with two tester beds and the result is slightly ludicrous. But, you can get both single and double field beds, and in either case, the bed forms a large part of the room decoration and so deserves detailed attention.

The old field beds are high from the floor; modern reproductions are lower, but in both cases it is customary to hide the bed frame and the space under the bed with a valance, skirt, or frill. This is usually made of the same fabric as the tester, and it was quite common in the old days to use that same material for the window curtains and perhaps one chair. This of course you cannot do if you use lacy tester material.

Late 17th Century bedchamber of wealthy Colonist. Note beautiful panelling, bed hangings and curtains of embroidered wool on cotton.

Two useful, attractive bedroom items with an old-time provincial look—
night stand and upholstered dressing table bench in maple.

The whole bed needs to be considered in planning the fabrics to use for the bedroom generally. There is the tester cover, the bedspread (quilt, counterpane, or coverlet) the valance and, in some early beds, the curtains or draperies over the head posts. In a great many bedrooms there will be sufficient plain background, or enough variety in pattern and color to withstand a tester, spread, and valance of the same fabric and pattern. The inside of the tester cover should of course be lined with plain material, and all pieces may well be edged with a solid color.

With a wide maple tester bed having turned posts, shaped head board, and no footboard (a fairly late type), using a gay calico or flowered chintz, with plenty of light background showing, the room could probably well stand an easy chair or chaise longue covered in the same material. Sometimes an equally good effect is secured by using plain, natural, or solid colored material for the bedspread to offset the gaily busy pattern of the tester and valance.

Another type of canopy bed that does not look too pretentious for these small Early American bedrooms is the angel bed. This has a very short canopy over the head of the bed. The canopy may be attached to the ceiling of a low room or the wall of a higher one. The usual depth is not more than two and a half to three feet. Simple canopies of this type can be made of thin wood over which fabric is stretched and glued. A frill or flounce, six or eight inches deep, is hung from the edges of the frame. The bed and canopy can be nicely tied together by a narrow width of material hung so as to form a curtain hanging down over each head post of the bed. These curtains extend a short distance along the sides of the canopy and are tied back at the post so that they do not interfere with air circulation, or stop access to the bedside tables.

One of the earliest canopy coverings for the field beds was a fish net stitch over a muslin backing. This makes an attractive canopy treatment today for a room keyed to the early 18th century. For a more feminine room, such as that of a young girl, a white lacy tester cover is ideal. The coverlet and valance however can be of a woven material, either flowered or plain, or even the old woven linen type decorated with a pattern in heavy cotton stitching, all in white. But for many rooms nothing looks more delightful and quaint than an early woven coverlet in the home-dyed colors. These bedspreads were made by hand in the 18th century from yarn spun and dyed at home. The favorite colors were blue, green, yellow, red, pink, and brown for the design on a white ground.

Another early type of spread that is suitable for use with lacy testers is the candlewick. These spreads can be used in plain white or in color, but they should not be of the obviously modern designs such as diamond tufts in color on white, or intricate geometric patterns. They have, as a consequence, to be chosen with care—and taste.

The other commonly used types of coverlets belong to the late 18th and early 19th centuries, and are known as pieced quilts and patchwork quilts. From these the name bed quilt is derived. The pieced quilt differs from the patchwork kind in that it is made entirely of small scraps of cloth stitched together to form one large piece. This piece, the size of the finished quilt, is then quilted to a backing of some other material in one or more layers. Sometimes a layer of cotton was inserted between the piecework and the backing.

In the patchwork quilt the small pieces of cloth are sewn separately onto the background material. Both types are equally effective in contributing to the old-time atmosphere of the bedroom. The modern, factory-produced quilts in imitation of these styles do not quite have the authentic air. In the case of woven coverlets, however, the machine-made products of some manufacturers are entirely satisfactory. But they must be of the best quality if they are not to look like cheap imitations.

In cases where it is desired to use a field bed in a room that is too low for it you can sometimes compromise by leaving off the tester, or you may replace the bowed tester with a flat one. If the posts terminate in spindles that fit into holes in the tester frame, you may be able to substitute turned finials for the spindles. In other cases, spindles and the finials that screw into them can be removed entirely without altogether spoiling the look of the posts.

The closest alternative to a field bed for a low room would be a tall-post bed with pineapple or other finials. These beds are really products of the last decade of the 18th century and of the first of the 19th. But because of their apparent kinship with the tester beds which were used well into the 19th century, they look equally antique.

The Revolutionary period saw the introduction of the short turned-post bed of which a great variety is available, both originals, and in reproduction, today. Many of them were made of maple, or maple-stained birch. Pine and the soft woods are not suitable for the more delicate turnings because the thin edges break off so easily. That is why turned pine bed posts are so much heavier in appearance.

The low-post beds of this simple provincial type are deservedly popular, and generally more satisfactory in creating an 18th century atmosphere than the later spool beds. In buying the original turned beds, however, if they have been modernized, it pays to see that the work has been properly done. The original beds were high off the floor, and too often the shortening of the legs has been done inexpertly and without consideration for appearances. Cut too low, these old beds seem obviously mutilated, a result that detracts very much from their antique appearance. The effects of this barbarism can sometimes be counteracted by the use of a bedrail valance or skirt, or even by having the coverlet hang well down both at the sides and bottom of the bed. Incidentally, pieced and patchwork quilts look better on these beds than they do on any others.

Early Bedroom Details

If the bedroom has a fireplace it will call for a hearthrug of some kind, and possibly a comfortable chair close by. A nice little wing chair in chintz or needlework, or even a more modern low-backed upholstered bedroom chair would not look amiss drawn up to the hearth. Some prefer a Windsor or rocker here, but it should not, in these small rooms, be of high, top-heavy construction. With some of the tall-post beds you may find that an early ladder-back arm chair of pine or maple looks well. It can have a cushion covered in some fabric that harmonizes with the bed coverings, but the actual material should not be the same. That would give it too much of a modern touch.

A favorite for the bedroom hearth is a small hooked rug of a primitive pattern, but the mottled woven rag rug is usually acceptable. If you use several such rugs they should be fairly small. One such on either side of the bed and a longer one at the foot is a common arrangement, even with an old chest at the foot of the bed. But if the bed is in a corner you may get a better balance by using a larger rug to one side, covering the center part of the floor. If this large rug is of the hooked variety it should preferably be of a geometric pattern. Primitive designs in the latter type of rug may be used provided they are not absolutely ugly.

On the whole, diamonds or squares, fern leaves or flowers have a more bedroomy effect than patterns of geese or dogs. The colors naturally must be selected to harmonize with the bed draperies and frills. Scatter rugs of the braided type, woven linen or cotton in solid colors, and even some of the more modern rugs, plain in color and short in tuft, are suitable for the Early American bedroom.

The floor itself may be of a plain waxed finish, or painted, or even spattered all over.

The fireplace andirons should be of black wrought iron—low, and small in scale. If the cupboards over the fireplace have exposed hinges, as they should, they are best painted the color of the woodwork.

In the provincial Colonial bedroom furnished with the later styles of maple, birch and walnut furniture of no particular period you can very well use wallpapers. But you must be sure that any paper you select will harmonize with the fabrics both as to color and design. They should not be very similar; but they should have the same period feel, and the scale of the patterns should not be too noticeably different. The size of the wallpaper pattern can generally be larger than that of the fabric because the paper design always looks smaller on the wall.

Fortunately we have a wide selection of papers to choose from. The more generally appropriate ones will be the simpler floral designs such as all-over natural roses. Where large areas of wall are visible an open pattern with a detached motive is generally best. For a big room you might very well use a fairly large pattern, and for a smaller room a tiny open pattern scattered over a soft white background. The design, in other words, should be scaled to the room.

A very good substitute for florals in these early bedrooms is one of the all-over patterns in a single color copied from an original early paper. These

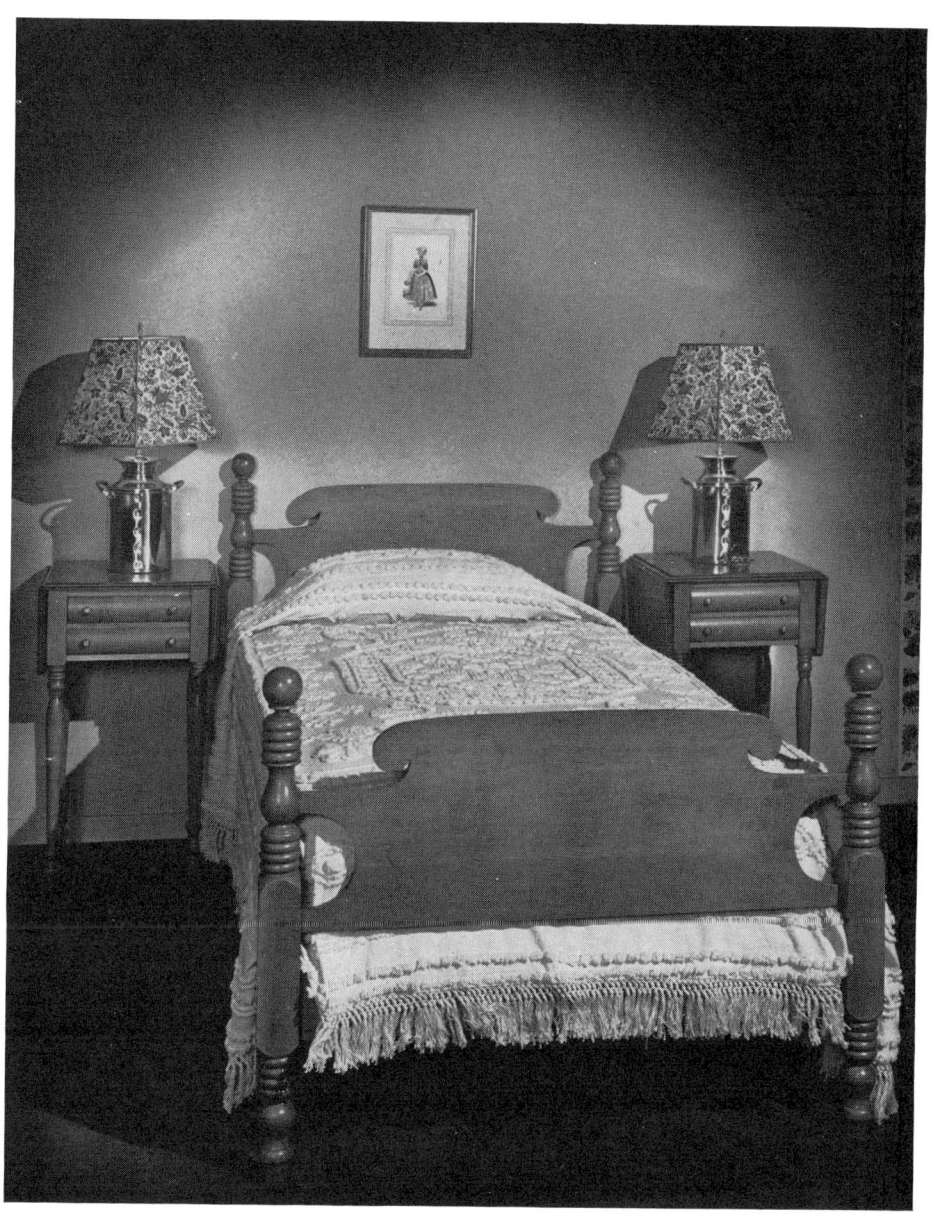

An early 19th Century ensemble of solid foot- and head-board bed with a pair of work stands serving as night tables.

A delightful serpentine-front dresser with a complementary mirror in mahogany and gilt.

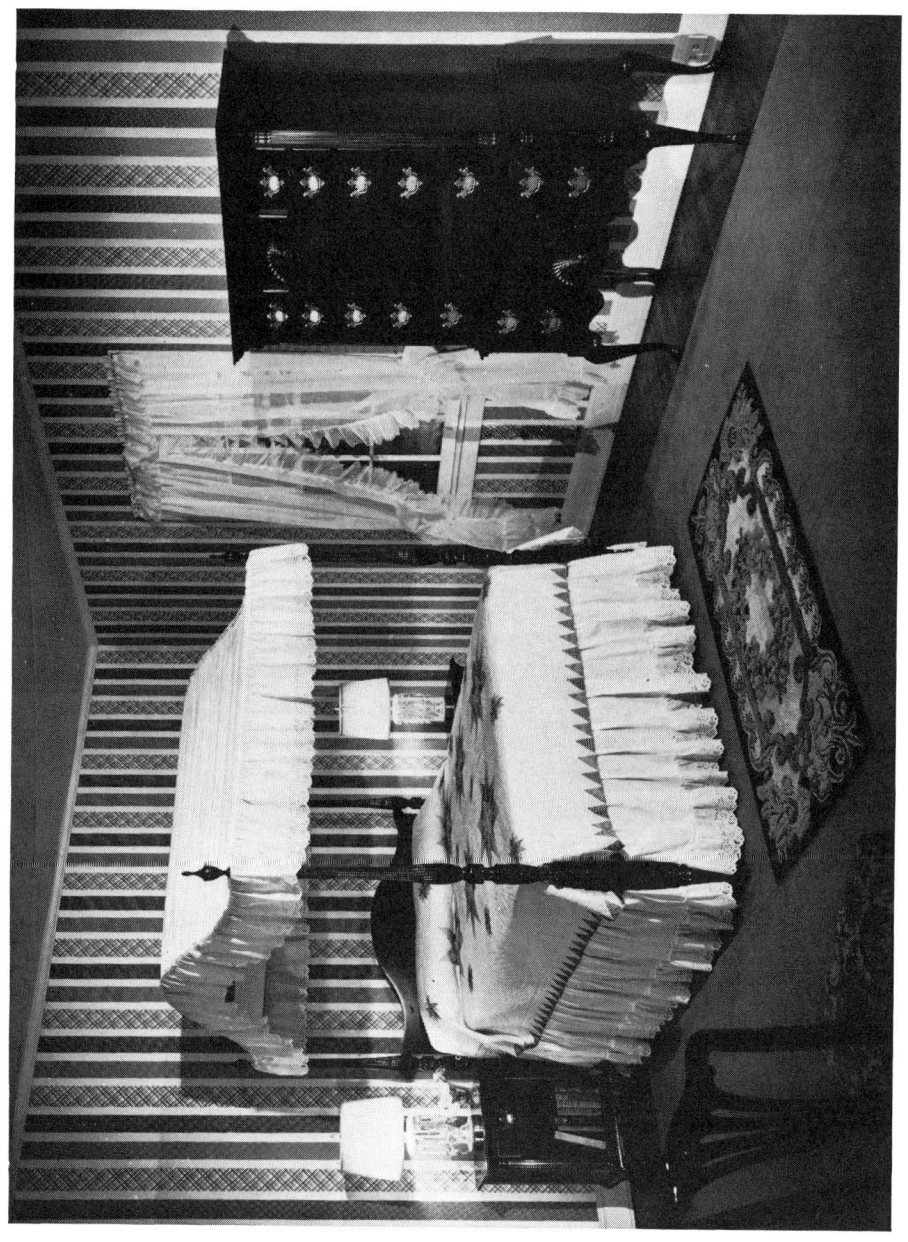

Twentieth Century adaptation of an 18th Century bedroom with tester bed and flat-top, Queen Anne type highboy; a more formal room.

are available in interesting blues or reds, and the overall effect is that of a heavy lace pattern on a colored background. An equally useful alternative is a natural flower in color inside a sort of scroll cartouche forming a light-colored background for it. These designs are arranged diagonally across the paper over a background composed of tiny stylized silhouetted flowerets on a deep-colored background. The effect is something like flowered cartouches appliqued on fishnet, but even more decorative. This is a type of paper obtainable in great variety, but the colors are all-important in creating the atmosphere we want.

For wall decoration samplers are very good, but any old print in a simple wood frame will be satisfactory, and an old looking glass on the wall will add to the antique air.

One of the determining factors in deciding upon the degree of formality in these early bedrooms will be the structural woodwork. In a very old house where the wall plates and the roof beams are exposed you need to concentrate on a primitive style. The plainer the bed, the more unpainted woodwork, and the simpler the floor coverings the better. Plaster walls should not be papered or tinted; all hardware should be iron; and the windows adorned with nothing more elaborate than India prints.

If the timbers are cased in you can go a step further and have painted woodwork, stenciled or spattered floors, rugs with more symmetrical flower designs or even braided rugs. The windows can have glass curtains (never crossed however), with printed calico draw curtains. If the hearth is of dark stone you can paint the fireplace brickwork dull black or apply black lead, provided not much brick is showing. A little elegance can be introduced through the use of andirons with brass finials.

In the earlier bedroom you can get a simple but pleasing effect by using a plain pine dressing table with turned legs and an old pine framed mirror over it. Some of these tables have a pair of drawers sitting on the flat top, and one or two large drawers in the apron. For bedside tables nothing looks better than one or a pair of old candlestands with tapering straight legs and one small drawer. They should be large enough to hold a lamp and a book or even a telephone if desired. In the more sophisticated room you might even use tripod tables in walnut or maple, but they are really best left for a later period.

Every bedroom intended to provide modern standards of comfort needs both drawer space and hanging space for clothing. In these old houses which have no closet space in the bedroom, a substitute must be found and we are almost forced to resort to a wardrobe. When the room is large enough

A more formal maple bedroom, the double dresser having a Hepple-white flavor and the bed adorned with pineapple finials. Note rocker.

to accommodate it, an old Dutch "kas," or a pine "hanging" cupboard can be used to advantage. Old pine wardrobes and kases are available but they are costly, and good reproductions of them can only be obtained from some of the highest class furniture manufacturers. But good pine cupboards, copied from an authentic design can be made up by local or country cabinet makers, and finished to look as though they had been around a long time. They are good either in natural wood or painted, and perhaps decorated in the old manner. Those with a drawer at the bottom are as a rule the most useful.

Drawer space can also be obtained through the use of one of a variety of old-style chests, but in the early Colonial room we cannot use anything too ornate. In the William-and-Mary and Queen Anne days even some of the less pretentious houses had a chest-on-frame or chest-on-chest for clothes, and even the William-and-Mary or Queen Anne lowboys which could be, and were, used as dressing tables, with maybe Queen Anne mirrors over them. These serve equally well today.

In many Early Colonial bedrooms it is often desirable to have a writing desk of some kind. For this purpose you have the choice of a small slant-top desk with three drawers, or a fall-front type also with drawers that can be used for clothing and linens. Any small old type chair would serve for the desk such as a ladder-back or light Windsor. Of course a turned fiddle-back chair or an early Queen Anne or Dutch transitional type of chair with a vase back and Spanish foot would be more in keeping with a kas.

If it is desired to introduce a chaise longue into a simple, early bedroom it should theoretically be of the wood-framed type similar to an early day-bed, preferably in pine, walnut, or maple. But in any bedroom, however early, that has bed and window fabrics of a decorative or patterned type, an upholstered chaise longue covered in a similar material will not seem particularly out of place. It will, from the mere fact of size, be subordinate to the bed, and perhaps even serve to give the room a feeling of balance that it otherwise would not have. That of course would largely depend upon the placing.

The artificial lighting of these early bedrooms calls for a pair of replica candlesticks for the dresser, in glass, pottery, or pewter, and a larger pair for the bedside stands. Sconces of course can be used on either side of the bed or over the mantelpiece. An iron candlestand type of light may also be needed for the chair or chaise longue.

Early Colonial Kitchens

In no other room of the Early American house is it necessary to do a more thorough job of creating an old-time atmosphere than in the kitchen. Here we have not only to furnish a room but to find a place for important items that are blatantly modern in every respect. In addition to furnishing, therefore, we have to do a great deal of disguising if we want this important room to harmonize with the rest of the house. Our first problem is to hide as much of the equipment as possible under an old-fashioned façade. The three dominant pieces of course are the sink, the refrigerator, and the stove. The sink we can hide pretty well by building a wooden cabinet around it. The refrigerator we enclose as much as possible by putting it in a wooden cabinet so that only the door is exposed.

The stove may be dealt with in any one of several ways depending upon the type—gas, oil, coal or electric—and the design. Sometimes we can take off the legs and build a cabinet under it, and perhaps around it, build cabinets on either side to form counters; mount it on a brick base, or enclose it in a sort of brick "fireplace," and so on. Usually it is possible also to put a hood over the stove, and perhaps incorporate an exhaust fan. The hood can be of polished copper, painted metal, or enameled wood. Such a hood should be pyramidal in shape and not the modern restaurant type.

With these pieces of equipment suppressed as far as possible we can turn our attention to the furnishing. We still stick to the white plaster background, or if we have wood boarding or paneling, that should be left in its natural state. If you decide to add wood boarding it should not be the rubbishy knotty pine, and it should be properly antiqued. For a somewhat later Early American kitchen you can paint the wood one of the old colors and use a style of furniture to suit. The blue-gray colors however always seem a little formal, and greens and yellows or even brown and yellow are to be preferred.

The floor can be left in natural wood, heavily waxed so that grease will not stain it. But almost as antique an air can be secured with a heavy linoleum in a natural tile pattern. A combination of browns and reds in the linoleum is good but there should be no violent contrasts. The dark brown and bright red combinations with light gray mortar lines should be avoided; they never will look old. No apparent joint is much better than an exaggerated one.

The total effect of the floor covering should be subdued, not striking, and it should be darker than the rest of the room to give an air of solidity.

In selecting a tile pattern it is desirable to scale the pattern to the room—do not use very small tiles in any kitchen. They should ordinarily be at least five inches square, and usually eight or nine inches is better. The tiny ones are more suitable for bathrooms.

Plastic tiles of the greaseproof type are equally as good as linoleum and often easier to lay. But the same rule as to color applies, though you can use the jaspé or slightly marbleized patterns which do not show dirt so readily. The principle to keep in mind is that the floor should give the impression of being composed of an old-time material such as wood or tile, brick or stone. Therefore you cannot get the antique effect with linoleums or plastics that imitate rugs or are inlaid with fanciful designs.

The general plan for the Colonial kitchen is to use as many authentic pieces of furniture as possible, and to make the built-in units conform to them in design and surface material. The units that lend themselves most readily are the dressers—Welsh, Pennsylvania, or provincial pine—and similar pieces, such as milk benches, wall cabinets, hanging shelves, spice cupboards, or chests. You might even include a food safe that is not too crude, a chest-on-frame, a buffet of oak or pine derived from the Jacobean style with large drawers and a long, flat top you can use as a table or counter. You also might find room for a small hutch table; a heavy round or oblong work table either with a solid top or drop leaves, and so on. From this assortment it is easy to choose a variety of pieces to perform all the functions necessary to a modern kitchen. Furthermore we can build in a number of these units and still have them look like the old pieces, provided they are properly antiqued.

If the kitchen of an Early American house is in a wing you will probably have plenty of room to use all the necessary pieces without overcrowding. You may also be able to use a center table for meals, with one of the late Colonial whale-oil lamps over it. Here a four-legged circular pine table is ideal. Upon this you can place a late 18th century lazy Susan as the occasion demands. Since the table will often be used as a working surface, it should be very solid, and for that reason pedestal types are not so satisfactory. Any one of the early oak or pine Pilgrim styles would be much better even if it had stretchers.

For seats you could use sturdy "captain's" chairs, but even with their very low backs it is possible they would have to be moved when the table was used as a working surface. Any of the lighter kitchen-type chairs might be preferable for that reason, including low-backed Windsors or even chairs of the early Hitchcock type, unpainted.

Sanitary, washable cloth wall coverings are especially suitable for kitch-
ens. The examples shown here are adaptable to the old-time room.

Antique wall boxes in numberless variety offer space for handy storage and provide welcome decorative notes in the Early American kitchen.

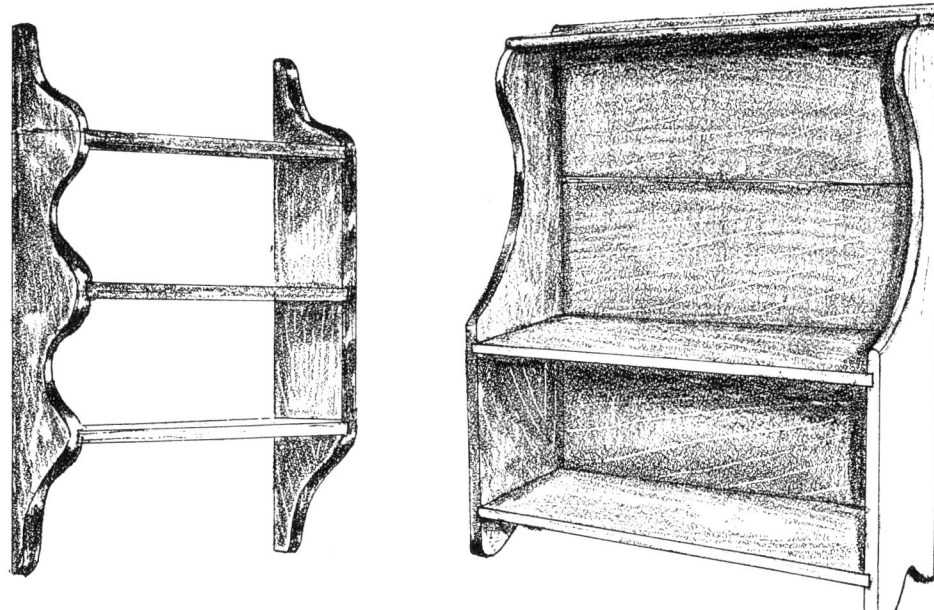

The hanging shelf and milk bench are equally at home in old-time kitchens.

In the oblong kitchen a trestle table is indicated. This should be of the sawbuck type which is more likely to be steady than the pillar trestle. Light arrow-back chairs or bamboo-turned Windsors can be moved in well under the table when not in use. Under no circumstances should the modern hewn "country" type of pine furniture be used in the old-time kitchen. Mere crudity is far removed from antiquity.

In arranging the kitchen furniture many of the modern ideas for efficiency and organization may be followed, but they should be held secondary to authentic appearance and general comfort. Ceiling cabinets should be avoided. Where accommodations of that type are essential, you can probably use separate 18th century hanging cabinets in natural wood or painted and decorated. The Welsh (or other) dresser will naturally be the major piece of furniture and it can be as large or as small as requirements demand. It can have various numbers and arrangements of cupboards and drawers, and the shelves can be used for the better dishes, arranged to display their color and beauty.

A standing cupboard with a raised-panel door or one of wide boards will serve for packaged food storage and cleaning materials. The interior can even be arranged to accommodate brooms, etc. Sink-side counters also provide storage space for pots and pans, and a dough trough with a drawer might provide a place to keep rarely used equipment, while the top serves as a stand for a toaster, waffle iron, teapot, coffee pot, or just growing plants under a window.

Spice chests on a wall are useful for holding modern tins of spices, nut-megs, or any of the numerous small objects used in the kitchen—skewers, toothpicks, etc. The top might form a shelf for the kitchen clock which of course should be of an early type, perhaps a shelf clock, and certainly not one in the form of a white-painted teapot trimmed with red roses! As in the early living room, wall boxes of various kinds can be used for decorative purposes, particularly spoon racks, knife and candle boxes. Painted tin trays also combine decorative value with utility.

Use of French Provincial Pieces

In almost any of these early rooms you can use one or more pieces of French Provincial furniture, providing it is of the simpler character. The natural wood chairs with rush seats have much the same feeling as the early Colonial ladderbacks. There are also some tables that can be used in the early Colonial room, but they should be plain and quite undecorated, with simple edges to the legs and top. The curved outlines of these pieces are not objectionable in these settings and actually may relieve the rigid feeling of a roomful of foursquare pieces and angular primitives.

13

FURNISHING THE GEORGIAN HOUSE: *The Georgian hall —Georgian living rooms—The Georgian dining room—The Georgian bedroom—Georgian kitchens.*

Chintz-covered wing chairs, books, printed calico curtains, iron floor lamps, rag rugs, random width plank floors, rush-seated side chairs, and white plaster walls are the properties with which we stage an illusion of elegant antiquity combined with modern comfort in the 18th century Early American house. In the Georgian house which is basically more formal, the chintzes may be replaced by damasks, the calico prints by brocaded floor-length draperies; Oriental carpets, painted paneling, and papered walls set off the fine period furniture in walnut and mahogany.

Between these two extremes lies the average small Georgian house that is every bit as informal in its own way as the later Early American domicile. Inherent in the architectural style, however, is a certain dignity and formality which needs to be considered in deciding on the furniture style. There are limits in informality beyond which we cannot go in the Georgian house without introducing a suspicion of incongruity. Pilgrim pieces will not do here, nor American Provincial. The selection of pieces for these small houses is therefore more or less confined to Jacobean, William-and-Mary, Queen Anne, Chippendale, Hepplewhite, and Sheraton with perhaps an odd item from Phyfe and French Provincial thrown in for good measure.

As we have already pointed out, only the larger houses or rooms are of a size to look well with the major furniture items of the William-and-Mary style. That is why we cannot do more than introduce an odd William-and-Mary piece into a room furnished in another period. Of all the styles mentioned, none can be better adapted to the less formal plan of furnishing than the Jacobean. Here you have oak furniture, generally very dark in finish. That finish helps to soften the ornamental features of certain pieces. The overall impression therefore is of a restrained dignity.

In seeking to establish an informal note in our small Georgian, however, we do not have to rely entirely on the Jacobean style. There are several other combinations of period styles that we can adopt, and odd pieces can be introduced to soften the severity of the room. The thing that we have to avoid in a Georgian setting is the use of crude pieces and provincial products that have no particular style at all. You do not get informality through lack of grace, or simple charm from the bizarre. Even in the Pilgrim era of course there were many pieces produced that have a feeling of informal dignity through the sheer honesty of their construction and happy choice of materials. Such pieces are quite at home in the smaller Georgian house provided the rest of the furniture and furnishings do not clash with them.

The one requirement that we have to insist upon today, especially in connection with modern reproductions, is that the quality be there. The furniture must obviously be well-made, and we want no "distressed" pieces purposely marred to give them the appearance of antiques. If a reproduction is hand-made from old wood and given a proper antique finish it will look old without being thrown downstairs or jumped on. And it is far better to have a frankly new copy of an old piece, than an obviously antique fake. After all, the worst thing that a reproduction piece can do is to make our room look just as it did when our antiques were new and our ancestors first used them.

The Georgian Hall

The entrance halls of Georgian houses, it will be recalled, extend from front to back through the center of the house. From this hall rises the main staircase, and from it open the doors to the rooms on either side. As in the case of the Early American entry, what we can do with this hall depends largely on its size, the location of the various doors opening from it, and the distance from the front door to the bottom of the stairs.

In the hall, unlike the entry, you have a vista, and space for floor furniture. You therefore have an opportunity of creating an air of space, and of treating that space like a room. Since most small halls have no windows around the door, and perhaps even no fanlight, an air of inviting brightness must be induced by the wall treatment. Imposing hallways are created by the use of architectural or block wallpapers, but in the small house these usually are oppressive, drawing the walls closer together, and absorbing too much light. For the informal hall they are not at all suitable.

Both plaster and wood walls are best painted an off-white, or the plaster may be finished in white and the woodwork in ivory or cream. If a paper is used it should have a detached motive with plenty of white, or at least a very light background, entirely unsophisticated and not dated by costumed figures or other such devices. No strong, dark pattern should be used at all. Whatever wall finish is adopted it gives a feeling of continuity and a sense of space if the same finish is carried on up the stairs.

An alternative to the wallpaper, and one which does not usually destroy the air of simplicity is a stencil border at dado height or at ceiling level, or even both, but this is generally best reserved for houses furnished in the later styles. For the more formal halls it might even be desirable to apply an allover stencil pattern. In such a case it is worthwhile to consider the use of a stencil wallpaper; then, if the results are not what you expected, you can at least remove the pattern without difficulty.

The hall floor should show a great deal of the wood, but if the flooring is not attractive it may be better to paint it or cover it with a linoleum of a solid color. As a rule a stencil border should not be used in a hall because it will make it look narrower, but an all-over stencil can take the place of linoleum. Only in the more formal halls should the black and white linoleum tiles be used. Except in some rare instances the use of colored tile effects is not desirable.

Whatever the floor finish, nothing looks better in the simply furnished hall than one or more hooked rugs properly placed. In some instances it is desirable to lay a small rug at each room door, with a large one near the front door. In other cases a long strip of hooked rug in the form of a runner is best, but there is often the problem of what to do when the foot of the stairs is reached. Probably the best solution is to use a wide runner in the main hall, placed along the center, and a narrow one alongside the stair, plus a similar one up the stairs. For a later and more sophisticated furnishing style, Oriental rugs can replace the hooked ones.

As regards the stairs, the more they can be tied in with the hall the better. In the simple houses the treads may be painted, with a dark paint "runner" up the center, or that center portion may be spattered. Otherwise the stair should be carpeted in the same manner as the hall. An interesting alternative would be to use a runner of cotton or linen, or a simulated homespun in a mottled effect.

The two essential pieces of furniture for the small Georgian hall are a table and a mirror. The least pretentious of all hall tables is not a table at all but a Pilgrim style chest, either carved or plain. The chest provides a flat top, and useful storage place for robes, blankets and other seasonal accessories. The higher chests, unfortunately, are usually big and therefore

Graceful English style tripod table of mahogany inlaid with boxwood.

out of scale for the small hall. In that case it is better to substitute an early type of table that is long in proportion to the width.

Extremely atmospheric are the 17th century pine-topped tables that have plenty of overhang, a long drawer, turned legs and a center stretcher. In the bigger hall a long, narrow refectory type table that has drawers is much more convenient. Very similar in appearance and equally acceptable is a Jacobean sideboard which has deep drawers, simple moldings and turned legs. Alternatives to the short table are an early chest-on-frame, a box table the top of which forms a lid, or a Pennsylvania table whose hall-marks are two drawers and center stretcher.

All of these tables call for an early type mirror, the simpler the better, preferably in a pine, oak, or walnut frame. Occasionally you may come across a simple courting mirror in a larger than ordinary size that will serve without creating an impression of formality.

Obviously it is impossible to list all the various combinations of furniture pieces that may be used in Georgian entrance halls to create a period atmosphere but we can catalog a few of them. In very many halls one or more chairs are a not inappropriate addition. For the earliest periods and the most informal houses, you might very well use tall banister backs or a simple wainscot chair. As a rule, the turned spindle type with rush seats is a little out of place.

For an 18th century hall you can use the chairs, tables and mirrors mentioned above, and for a slightly more formal air introduce a William-and-Mary or Queen Anne lowboy paired off with a Queen Anne type tall mirror. For this same period you can add a tall clock of the grandfather type. As the 18th century proceeds you might substitute a tripod candlestand for the table and a Windsor settee for the chair, using a scrollwork, crested walnut mirror.

In a hall of the transitional period you could use a Philadelphia Chippendale lowboy with a gilded walnut or mahogany mirror, and so enter the Chippendale period proper. At this time it would be quite in order to use a four-foot-high grandmother clock and one of a variety of Chippendale tables and matching mirrors.

Some of the card tables of this era, with one leaf that lifts up against the wall, are very effective in halls, but do not forget that the mirror has to go above the raised leaf. These tables are made in Chippendale, Hepplewhite, and Sheraton styles, some simple and some quite ornate. A chair of the same style, or for that matter any one of the three styles that looks well with the table, may be a useful as well as ornamental addition to the hall.

Lighting in the hall is a problem that is not always easy to handle. The inverted glass bowl type of fixture, that in the old days held a candle, is neither formal nor informal, but for the unpretentious hall wall sconces usually constitute less of a jarring note. The quillwork type or the earlier forms of girandoles are slightly more formal but they do add an antique note that is helpful.

Then there are square lanterns with glass sides, and the candle bracket type of sconces with glass chimneys. But the tall table lamps actually are more effective than either sconces or lanterns in preserving an 18th century air. A few real candles in tall brass candlesticks decorating the hall table also help in the illusion. In the more sophisticated halls the brass lanterns, either square or round, with plain or decorated glass, are quite satisfactory.

Georgian Living Rooms

Probably the most satisfactory of any room to furnish in Colonial style is the small Georgian living room. For one thing you have a tremendous range of materials and pieces to choose from and you can use really lovely things without being stifled by formality or bogging down in Victorian sentimentality.

Even in the smaller Georgian houses the rooms are usually large enough to contain everything for modern living and accommodate furniture built on a generous scale. And when such rooms are completed, if the planning is right, there will be ample comfort, old-time charm, and still plenty of space to satisfy our modern craving for air and light and absence of clutter.

It is in these rooms that we observe most clearly how accessories can influence the degree of formality. In two Georgian living rooms furnished practically alike, a rug may make all the difference between a feeling of ordinary comfort and a feeling of luxury. Apart from that it is the choice of the individual pieces that sets the keynote and many subtle changes can be effected by substituting one kind of piece for another.

Happily, comfort was the goal of most 18th century furniture designers and the results of their efforts combine very nicely with many of the comfortable furniture designs of the 20th century—the overstuffed sofas and chairs and love seats. Nevertheless it is just as well to make use of the early designs of upholstered pieces whenever possible; a large proportion of them, dating from Chippendale on, were extremely comfortable even by modern standards though they may not appear to be so because they are not so extravagantly padded.

In the smallest and least pretentious of our Georgian living rooms we can have our modern sofa or love seat. The only proviso is that we clothe it in a material reminiscent of the earlier days. There is always chintz which can be had in old-time patterns and adaptations of them. We can use cotton or linen weaves in old patterns and colors, or even homespuns, and we can use slipcovers with or without shirred ruffles, or make the same piece formal by dressing it up with box pleats.

For the more formal rooms the upholstery material may be a damask, brocade, or brocatelle, or indeed any modern fabric that has the color and texture and a pattern reminiscent of the 18th century materials. Of course we do not actually need to introduce modern pieces into these early rooms, for by 1710, we could have had wing chairs and upholstered sofas and love seats, though we have to admit few of them look as informal as some modern styles.

Strangely enough the style of a sofa does not have as much influence on the apparent antiquity of a room as does the material with which it is covered. Almost any of the commoner styles of sofa made today, except the rigidly angular modernistic ones, can be incorporated in a Georgian room without spoiling its authentic air of age and homogeneity provided the fabric is right and the design good. Borax pieces of course do not look good anywhere.

In point of period you can start as far back as William-and-Mary, or even persuade some oak Jacobean or Carolean pieces to look carelessly informal. Indeed there are pieces like the Jacobean gateleg table with twisted legs that make themselves at home with many other styles. You can have the walnut of Queen Anne alongside mahogany Chippendale, and in some rooms even introduce inlaid pieces of Hepplewhite or Sheraton to relieve the monotony of plain mahogany and cabriole curves.

In the small room with an early Georgian feeling you might well start with Queen Anne—say a high-backed roll-arm sofa with three cabriole legs at the front. That would be the principal upholstered piece. With a fireplace you could use one or a pair of wing chairs with cabriole legs, stretchers, and loose cushions.

For one end table you could use an 18th century lamp table with smoothly turned and tapered legs and spoon feet, with a molded and scalloped apron. For variety you might install at the other end a low etagère, or a book stand of the English Regency type, or perhaps a Queen Anne tea table with tiny drop leaves at the ends. The tea table, incidentally, mounted on flat, pillar type legs, makes an excellent coffee table. Large tables of ex-

The tier table, though not common, is useful in crowded corners for display of small objects, or as an auxiliary serving stand at tea time.

Georgian-type living room arrangement of four useful tables: end table with shelves, coffee table, tier table, nest of three occasional tables.

Adaptations such as this vanity, usable also as a living room or hallway desk, combine olden charm and beauty with sleek modernity.

actly the same design are often used as sofa tables. Large or small, they all have useful drawers.

A "must" in the majority of today's living rooms is a bookcase. Often the shelves are built in, but this has the disadvantage of making it difficult to rearrange the furniture in a small room. But whether the bookcase is a piece of furniture or a set of fixed shelves it should not be located between windows. A handsome bookcase and the spines of the books it contains should always be where daylight can strike them. Between windows the light is in the eyes during the daytime and the books in comparative darkness, and the piece of furniture loses its decorative value.

Since a writing table or desk will also be a necessity in the living room it is a good thing to combine it with a bookcase. In a room that is high enough —and most of the Georgian house rooms are—the answer is a secretary, a piece of furniture that is available in seemingly endless variety. Today it is possible to buy scaled down reproductions of secretaries in walnut or mahogany that can be used in the smaller rooms. In many living rooms the glass-fronted secretary will be a too-imposing piece, overpowering the rest of the furniture. The obvious thing to do here is to substitute a slant-top desk and put the books on hanging shelves or in a standing bookcase.

The slant-tops range from the simple desk-on-frame to the serpentine fronted type with deep drawers on bracket feet, or the even more luxurious block-front with claw-and-ball feet. The flat-fronted type on bracket feet is probably the most unpretentious of all designs, even if it is made in burl walnut. One thing to observe here is that several sets of tall cabriole legs in a small room are likely to prove both monotonous and disturbing. Even an older style of ball- or bun-foot desk may be preferable to even the rudimentary cabrioles that you get on a desk made up from a detachable desk box set on a lowboy.

Since most of the pieces we have talked about so far are commonly of walnut, added interest would be gained by introducing a piece in apple wood or even dark pine, always supposing that the quality is equal to that of the rest of the furniture.

For the books there are simple pieces consisting of open shelves with a drawer or cabinet below. Included in this class are several Hepplewhite designs of book shelves that are quite at home in an early 18th century room. It is also possible to use an English style etagère with spindle type shelf supports, but you need some kind of end support for the books. The simplest and most effective support is a piece of painted tin bent at right angles and tucked under the book ends. If this furniture is in a brown ma-

The top section of this block-front secretary can be removed to form a low desk if the height seems too imposing for its surroundings.

Quite elegant but delightfully appealing is the French Provincial desk, equally at home in living room, bed chamber or small library.

hogany and not inlaid so much the better. The etagère shelves, being large
and square, can be used for magazines; otherwise a magazine rack or Can-
terbury (originally designed to hold sheet music) can be substituted.

For side chairs in this early Georgian living room you might well
adopt the spoon-backed Queen Anne type, and cover their rush seats with
loose cushions. Even better would be the same type of chair with an upholstered seat in haircloth or leather. In more formal rooms the seats would be
upholstered in needlepoint, though it would be possible to substitute a plain
covering in a modern diagonal weave without spoiling the effect.

Since this room would be predominantly late Queen Anne in feeling,
and quite on the informal side, the floor covering should be restricted to
either a braided rug or possibly a reproduction of a Chinese rug such as
might have been imported by the traders of Salem.

For a Georgian living room more reminiscent of the mid-18th century
some of the walnut pieces would be replaced by mahogany of the pre-Chippendale era. You could still keep your Queen Anne tilt-top tables and similar small walnut pieces; they would add the spice of variety to a mahogany
setting. The sofa, however, might be an early Georgian high-backed type
with flared wings and six legs, three of which would be cabrioles.

Probably more comfort would be secured through the substitution
of a frankly Chippendale sofa with a loose cushion and altogether deeper
upholstery, but in neither case would this piece of furniture be of the kind
that extends an invitation to the weary soul to recline. Both are innately
dignified, however simply upholstered or slip-covered, and if you want a
room that caters only to the lazy and the tired, a more modern sofa would
be a better choice. Both the Lawson and Tuxedo styles have much to recommend them in the informal Georgian room.

In the case of a really small room many people prefer to substitute a
love-seat, or even a pair of them, for the sofa. The Chippendale designs
with square legs and stretcher base would be appropriate here. A less rigid
pattern would result through substituting a wing chair with claw-and-ball
feet for one of the love-seats. With this the logical accompaniment would
be a small piecrust table, but with the Chippendale sofa you could use a less
decorative coffee table of the plainer Queen Anne style. The end tables
could be a pair of Sheraton book tables, foursquare and forthright whose
only concession to ornament would be fluted tapered legs below the bottom
shelf.

The writing desk could be a much lighter piece than the multiple-
drawered slant-top. Many people prefer a writing table or lady's writing

Magnificent breakfront secretary-bookcase in light pine. Used in a room with proportions as impressive as its own, it is a truly dramatic piece.

In bedroom, living room or hall, a Philadelphia highboy such as this lends both distinction and charm to its background.

desk for living room use. A good compromise is a secretary desk, though these are usually of a somewhat later period. Some Sheraton types with sliding tambour doors and a folding top look well in an Early Chippendale room, though most of them have a certain amount of inlay. There is also a particular style of Hepplewhite tub chair that is quite appropriate for use with this desk. The arm supports and legs form a continuous flowing curve reminiscent of the curves of a cabriole leg but even more graceful.

The side chairs in this room should be of the less elaborate Chippendale forms. A particularly good combination might be achieved through the use of a simple pierced-splat pattern chair that was made of maple around 1760. This had straight legs and stretchers, with a padded seat let in. Another simple pattern was the Chippendale ladder-back style with a rounded top.

For larger rooms you can of course indulge in more elaborate pieces, including perhaps a small breakfront bookcase with a center dropleaf that forms a writing desk. But however elaborate or simple the living room is to be, it will gain in interest if two or more sympathetic styles are mixed and variety attained in the woods that are used without the differences being too obvious. Hepplewhite, Chippendale, and Sheraton styles all offer pieces that can be combined with happy results. Even a piece or two of French Provincial of Louis XV flavor may be included, provided judgment and good taste are exercised.

In all of these later 18th century rooms the most popular floor covering by far is the Oriental rug. But hooked rugs with a formal pattern can also be used, as well as most solid-color carpets in pile weaves.

The living room walls in the small Georgian house may be either painted or papered. The earlier the room the more suitable will be a paint finish for which any of the much-advertised Williamsburg colors or the colors previously mentioned in connection with Early American houses can be used. This applies to the plastered walls just as much as it does to the boarded or paneled ones. Incidentally, if the plaster is painted it will be quite authentic to use a different color on one of the walls.

In place of the paint the plaster walls can be covered with a suitable wallpaper. For the simple rooms this could be one of the dainty chintz papers or a toile de Jouy reproduction. Both geometric and floral patterns also are used, and quite a rich effect is secured with papers resembling the early damasks and brocaded velvets.

With Chinese Chippendale furniture predominating you can use papers with an Oriental feeling, together with lamps of Chinese porcelain, or English pottery with Chinese motives. Other lighting fixtures appropriate to the Georgian era are elaborate wall sconces of silver and glass, candlesticks with hurricane globes, and table lamps of glass or porcelain with shades of silk, parchment, fabrics, or even paper.

The floor-lamp standards should be of brass, bronze, copper or cabinet woods, though the dressier styles of black iron are permissible. The fireplace accessories, not including the tapestry pole screens of course, may be of brass, and with the small fireplace a brass fender may be added.

On the Early Georgian living room walls oil portraits are always good but with later styles of furniture a variety of imported prints, old maps, silhouettes, mezzotints, botany prints, and oil landscapes may be added. Shelf clocks, banjo clocks, and the rich-looking 18th century mahogany bracket clock are the most suitable types of timepieces.

The informal room would have windows hung with brocades or similar materials, of sill length, and a plain valance board over them. The room would gain in formality if the draperies were extended to the floor and the valance covered with the same material, possibly edged with ball fringe or other decoration. For the later room Venetian blinds are quite in order; they were introduced in America around 1767!

The Georgian Dining Room

In general the Georgian dining room follows the same furnishing plan as the living room in respect to types and mixtures of pieces, and the wall finishes. An exception is the floor which usually should have a rug large enough to go under the table and the chairs around it. If a rug of a very large size is used there should be one and a half to two and a half feet of bare floor around it, depending upon the size of the room.

This is one room in which it is desirable to have a certain amount of matching furniture. The chairs around the table should at least be alike, though they need not be of the same style or period as the table. In the informal house they can be of the Queen Anne style with rush seats, but in a more formal setting they would need to be pre-Chippendale or Chippendale of walnut or mahogany with upholstered seats.

The table can be a walnut or mahogany extension type, called a draw table; a large gateleg; or a pedestal design. The pedestal type is deservedly popular because there are no peripheral legs to get in the way of people seated around the board.

In furnishing the dining room we again have the opportunity of choosing any one of a number of delightful pieces of various periods. But most

This reproduction dining room group shows modern adaptations that preserve the elegant, carefully made appearance of the originals.

of us end up with a highboy of some sort which is wonderful for storing linens. For serving purposes and the storage of silver and glassware we may have a sideboard, or a lowboy if the room is small, or be content with one or more side tables with drawers.

The limit in elegance is reached with a serpentine or bow-fronted sideboard of the Hepplewhite or Sheraton styles. Excellent storage space is also provided by a corner cupboard or wall cupboard, or a late style of china closet.

For lighting we might have wall sconces of the living room type or even more fancy ones decorated with crystal prisms. Candlesticks and candelabra would adorn the sideboard, buffet, mantel, and table, and the ultimate in luxury would be attained with a crystal chandelier resplendent over a table bright with chased silverware, sparkling glass, and glistening napery.

The Georgian dining room, formal or informal, calls for very little in the way of wall adornment. Plain walls for simple houses, painted or papered for the more stylish ones, but very few pictures in any of them, and perhaps no more than one mirror. Lighting sconces and mantel ornaments, the display of silver and china in cupboards or on the sideboard inject all the color and decoration that the average room needs.

The windows follow the same pattern as the living room as do the upholstered pieces. The dining room quite often is even more formal than the living room.

The Georgian Bedroom

Most houses have more than one bedroom, and each bedroom can be furnished and decorated without reference to the other, and usually with no other consideration than the tastes and wishes of the member of the family who occupies it. Guest bedrooms are of course a special problem, but ordinarily they call for no more than tasteful period furnishing and decorating in subdued and restful tones. Otherwise in almost any house no two bedrooms will be alike, but they do, or should, have certain things in common. They should be quiet and restful; dark rooms should be lightened with bright colors and sunny rooms made to seem cheerfully cool with greens and blues. Masculine rooms call for bolder fabrics and wallpapers; feminine rooms for light patterns. The same principle carries over into the furniture.

Choice of pieces begins with deciding upon the bed which may be a low-poster, a high-poster, or a canopy type. The low post bed with turned and reeded posts and blanket rail and pineapple finials is a popular style that can be masculine or feminine according to the way it is dressed.

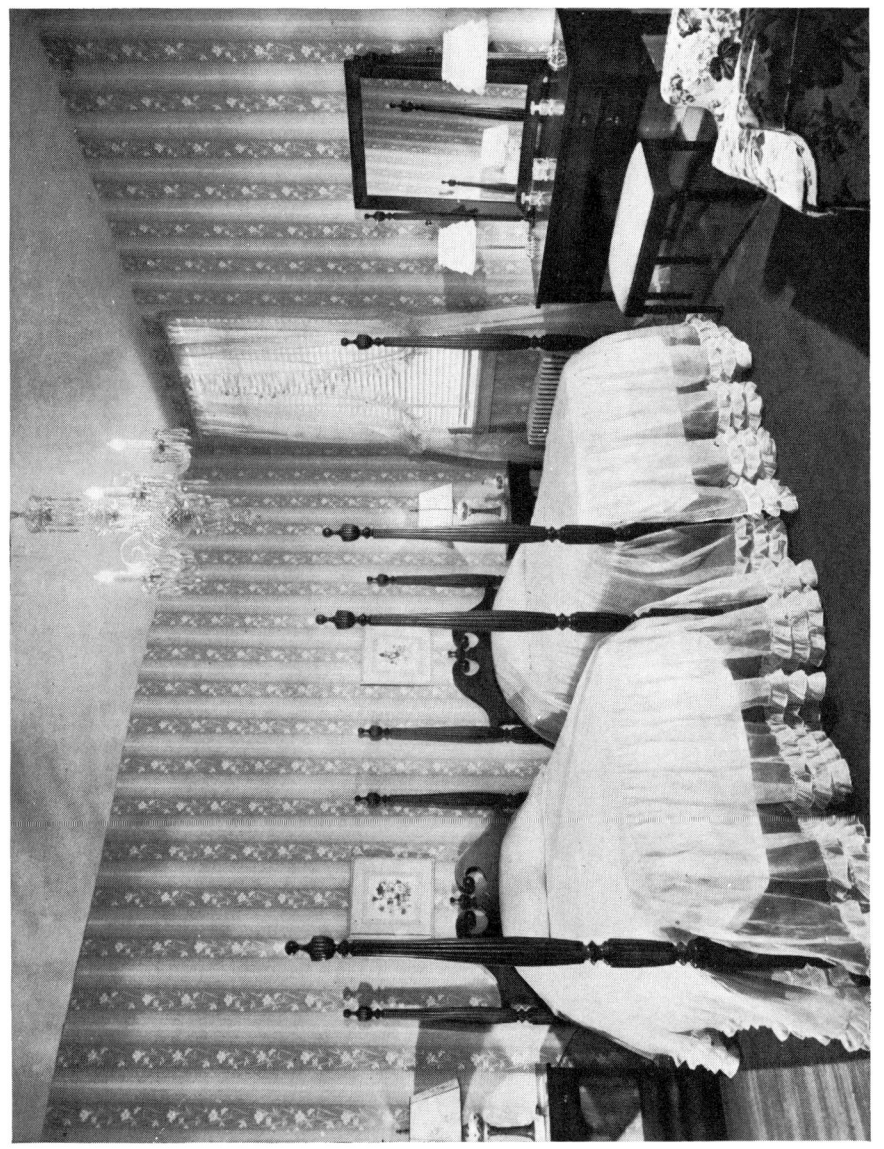

Two high-post beds in a bed chamber where twin tester beds could not be contained. Individual pieces and accessories are well related.

The twin beds in this up-to-date bedroom borrow the 19th Century arrow-motive; the chest has brasses of the middle 18th Century.

Any of the tester type beds discussed under Early American house furnishing can be used, but the primitive and provincial coverlets will be quite out of place in the Georgian bedroom. In the later bedrooms we can adopt more formal types of beds such as those with wooden canopy frames, perhaps with the frame decoratively painted, and posts with cabriole legs. The bedspreads for these might consist of appliqué chintz or white embroidery to match the valance, or a dimity or dotted Swiss valance with a candlewick spread. An extremely formal canopied bed results when carved posts are surmounted by a scalloped and quilted tester.

A low four-post bed is much less formal than the tester bed, and is of proportionately less importance in influencing the character of a room. The low post nevertheless can be adorned with the same kind of spreads and rail valances and thereby made more masculine or feminine as the case may be.

The dressing table is another important unit determining the character of the bedroom. In the small Georgian house it can be almost any kind of a table or similar flat-topped piece. The only requirements are that it be of a convenient height and equipped with drawers and a mirror. Small knee-hole desks, either square or kidney-shaped, lowboys of the William-and-Mary or Philadelphia Chippendale styles, small block-fronts, English tea tables, powder tables, and even French Provincial game tables have been adapted for the purpose since dressing tables were introduced around 1700 or so.

Today we can get adaptations of these pieces in Chippendale, Sheraton, Hepplewhite, and French Provincial styles, and practically every one of them will add grace to a mid-18th century bedroom. Powder tables, or *poudreuses* as the antiquarians love to call them, are the only type of 18th century dressing tables that have a mirror attached. Usually the powder table mirror is made to fold down and form the top of a center compartment. For all other dressing tables the mirror must be hung on the wall, unless it is mounted on a separate drawer or stand. The mirror, naturally, would be of the same style as the table.

A dressing table seat, which is so often moved about and adjusted in use, should be light and small and preferably low-backed. Most good reproductions of period dressing tables are made with chairs to match for this reason, and that is generally the best solution in preserving a period atmosphere. Some, of course, prefer stools or backless seats for dressing table use. Various styles of these are available as period pieces. Some of them are called long stools or window seats and both kinds have arms at each end.

Then there are the small round or square stools with upholstered tops. Some of them have exposed frames and legs while other equally popular ones show no woodwork at all. This last type brings up again the whole subject of dressing tables and seats and their contributions to period rooms.

Most bedrooms of feminine inspiration have voluminous bed and window draperies, curtains, valances, et cetera, so that fabrics form nine tenths of the decorating, and the wooden pieces are inundated under a froth of frills. In such a bedroom it is actually the fabrics rather than the furniture pieces that set the period. If the fabrics are of the authentic types, or modern derivations that have the character and pattern of the old-time materials we can still have our period room. Therefore it should not be surprising that we can take a modern glass-topped table and dress it in muslin or organdy and have it fit into a period room. The same thing applies to the dressing table stool. This is one of the few instances in which we can cheat on the rules for decorating period rooms and get away with it!

Besides the bed and madame's dressing table, the master bedroom also needs a dresser for the master. This can be any of the low dressers or chests of drawers with a dressing mirror on top. The dressing mirror is a small, swinging, looking glass mounted on a drawer or drawers, and such mirrors are just as useful, though perhaps not as fashionable, today as they were two hundred years ago. And they do add a period note to the bedroom in which they are used.

If there is still space in our Georgian bedroom we can perhaps find a place for a bonnet-top tallboy, highboy, or chest-on-chest. This will give us all the extra drawer space we possibly can need without taking up a lot of floor space. Simple square-topped candlestands will no longer serve as bedside tables. The Georgian bedroom calls for more substantial pieces, usually with two or three drawers. All the leading designers made such pieces, and replicas are available today.

In all these bedrooms, formal or informal, feminine or masculine, a nicely finished natural wood floor is generally richest and best. But the boards must be fairly evenly matched and smooth, and have a well-cared for look. If the floor is not good, its defects may be covered by paint, and the paint can be used as a ground for stencil decoration or spattering. This also is a good way to get color into a bedroom trimmed wholly in white.

An acceptable, and sometimes preferable, substitute for paint is cork or linoleum. If the latter, it should always be of the rich and heavy type that will not show every inequality of the surface beneath it. Solid colors are best for Georgian bedrooms, dark greens and browns especially, and always darker than the walls. The choice of color of course will be influenced by the colors of the small rugs that will be used by the bed and dressing table and in front of the fireplace, if there is one. These can be hooked rugs in subdued floral patterns, or solid-color linen weaves.

Georgian Kitchens

Although in the Georgian era mahogany was the favored cabinet wood we do not need to use it in the kitchen. This is one room in the house where the material from which the furniture is made is strictly subordinate to its functions, and where simplicity is desirable regardless of the splendor and elegance of the rest of the house. Therefore little needs to be said here regarding the Georgian kitchen that we have not already mentioned in connection with the Early American kitchen. Pine is still the favored wood, though Jacobean oak can sometimes be substituted. Another deviation might be in the direction of painted furniture.

Cupboards, dressers, dough troughs, tables and chairs can take their cue from the Sheraton fancy chairs and Pennsylvania Dutch decorated pieces. Some of the later Hitchcock chairs, with their black-red paint, gilding, and stencilwork can be teamed with other painted pieces to make a gay and lively kitchen that is reminiscent of an earlier age. The tendency here unfortunately is to overdo the decoration. A single, odd, painted piece among others of natural wood enhances both. Even a set of Hitchcock chairs around a plain pine table gains from the evident restraint that has obviously been exercised. Restraint in decoration of course is evidence of innate good taste, as it is in manners and even morals!

POSTSCRIPT

Seven years before the end of the 18th century the separation between the mother country and the American states became complete. Furniture makers continued to use the designs of Chippendale, Hepplewhite and Sheraton, but Phyfe was leading the trend to Federal styles. The eagle displaced Chippendale's rook, and stars took the place of gilt balls. France became the favorite source of inspiration. For long years Phyfe's creations graced the parlors and dining rooms of the well-to-do and socially important. But many of the things he made were soon found to be also suitable for the smaller homes. His products were more sturdy and less formal in design than those of the English cabinetmakers, and therefore more suitable to the unpretentious house.

Today they are even more popular in middle-class American homes, but a great deal of modern furniture in this style is poor indeed. That is why discriminating homemakers are shying away from Duncan Phyfe, and even Phyfe addicts are learning that the judicious mixture of a little Sheraton, Early Empire, or even a Victorian piece or two will give their rooms more character and interest, and make the house look as though it had grown—instead of the furniture being bought *en masse* on a Saturday night spree. That indeed is the way to create a home, whether it is old or new in spirit, whether it is housed in a dwelling that was raised 200 years ago, or in one that was built last week.

A GLOSSARY OF
HOUSE AND FURNITURE TERMS

Acanthus. A conventionalized leaf motive from the acanthus bush, used on furniture; originating with the Greeks.

Adam, Robert. 1728–1792. Best known of the Adam brothers, architects and designers of everything that went into a house. Scottish by birth, but worked in London from 1758.

American Provincial furniture. Country styles of utilitarian furniture.

Apron. A flat wood strip below a chair seat or table top to connect top and legs.

Argand lamp. An oil lamp with a circular hollow wick to improve combustion and give better light. Invented by a Swiss named Argand in 1783.

Arrow-back chair. A chair with a back made of arrow-shaped spindles, Federal period.

Aubusson rug. A woven tapestry rug made in Aubusson, France.

Axminster rug. A commercially made rug with pile; comes in all widths and gives good service. Name originated in Axminster, England.

Bake oven. The small oven found in the rear or at the side of the kitchen fireplace in an Early American house.

Ball foot. Spherical base of furniture leg.

Banding. An inlay used for decoration, frequently of contrasting color or grain.

Banister-back chair. One with flat back slats running vertically between upper and lower rails; slats are usually split turnings with the flat side forward.

Banjo clock. So-called because of the shape of its case. Invented by Simon Willard in 1802.

Baseboard. Wide board running around the room at the base of the wall and touching the floor.

Batten door. A door in which the vertical boards are fastened together by nailing horizontal ones across them.

Beading. Small half round molding, generally used as a finish to a plain surface.

Bench. A plain wooden backless seat for two or more.

Betty lamp. Early type of dish-shaped lamp made of tin or iron, with homemade wick, burning oil.

Block-front. Recessed center panels between projecting sections. 18th century method of decorative construction for bookcases, desks, etc.

Borax furniture. Flashy, tasteless furniture, cheaply made.

Bow front. A convex shaped front, characteristic of much 18th century furniture.

Bracket feet. A right angle corner support with a curved inner edge in bracket form. Used on 18th century chests, desks, cabinets and cupboards.

Breakfront. A bookcase or cabinet in which the center part projects further than the two side sections.

Brewster chair. A chair with a wooden seat, many turned spindles, and a heavy turned frame. A piece of Pilgrim furniture said to have belonged to Elder Brewster, one of the early rulers of the Plymouth Colony.

Brocade. An upholstery or drapery fabric of fine quality with a raised woven design, sometimes with a gold or silver thread worked through it.

Brocatelle. Heavy fabric in which woven large patterns appear embossed.

Broken pediment. One which is interrupted in center to make space for some type of decoration. May be either a swan's neck, goose neck, or straight-edged break.

Bun foot. A ball foot, slightly flattened, found on William-and-Mary furniture.

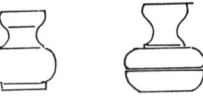

Butler's tray. A tray whose four sides fold down on hinges to serve as a table when it is placed on a stand.

Butterfly table. A drop-leaf table, round, square, or oval, with turned legs, whose leaves are supported by brackets resembling butterfly wings. First made in Connecticut about 1700.

Cabriole (bandy) leg. One which curves out at the top to form a knee, continuing down in a curving taper, and bending out to form a foot.

Camphene. A mixture of alcohol and turpentine, burned in lamps.

Candle sconce. A small shelf of metal or wood for holding candle, having a back and sometimes narrow sides, and perhaps a reflector.

Candlewick. Tufting of cotton used for decorative purposes on a bedspread, or possibly draperies.

Canopy. A covering suspended over a bed.

Captain's chair. A low, round-backed wooden chair with splayed turned legs and stretchers, and shaped wooden seat. So named for its use by sea captains.

Carolean Period. 1660–1685. English. Reign of Charles II.

Cartouche. An ornament in the form of a scroll partly unrolled, used as a motive on cabinets and other pieces.

Carver chair. A turned chair with sturdy frame, rush seat, spindle back. One of the earliest types of American chairs said to have been brought here by Governor Carver of the Massachusetts Bay Colony.

Cased-in timbers. Beams that have been covered with boarding to improve their appearance.

Cellarette. A small storage container or cabinet for wine and spirit bottles; a deep drawer in a sideboard for the same purpose.

Chair rail. A horizontal strip of wood placed about sill height on a wall to prevent marring by a chair back; also sometimes formed by the dado cap.

Chaise longue. French for long chair or daybed or a form of sofa with pillow support at one end, but no back.

Chippendale, Thomas. 1718–1779. Most famous of all English cabinetmakers, who developed the furniture styles that bear his name.

Claw-and-ball-foot. End of a furniture leg in the form of a bird's claw grasping a ball. Originally a dragon's claw holding a pearl (Chinese mythology).

Club foot. A foot shaped like the end of a club, with a thick, flat base.

Cockle-shell decoration. Same as scallop shell. Carved shell ornament, common on Queen Anne, Chippendale, and Louis XV furniture.

Comb-back Windsor. One in which several spindles of the chair back extend upward to form a comb-shaped top. A second, smaller comb will sometimes be found above the other.

Commode. A low chest or cabinet, with doors or drawers, used against a wall.

Console. A small side table over which a mirror is usually hung. Originally a bracket type table with S-shaped leg, standing under a pier glass.

Cornice. Horizontal molding across the top of a piece of furniture, or at top of window.

Court cupboard. A double bodied cabinet used to hold plates, eating utensils, etc.

Cranberry glass. Glass the color of cranberries—red.

Credenza (credence). Side table or sideboard of special form.

Crewel embroidery. Where the design is worked on a cotton or linen background, in wool; an all-over pattern in variegated colors.

Cromwellian. 1649–1660. English furniture style; modified, undecorated Jacobean.

Crown glass. Window glass blown and whirled till it forms a sheet in the center of which is the thickened part, called the bull's eye. An alkali-lime glass similar in composition.

Cup turned leg. Turning on a leg that resembles an inverted cup.

Currier and Ives print. Popular lithographs in color depicting American life from 1840–1880.

Cyma curve. A simple double reversing curve.

Dado. A section of a wall below the chair rail that is treated in a different manner than that above the rail.

Daybed. Usually of cane, with 6 or 8 legs, and head rest that sometimes was let back and held in place with chains. Forerunner of chaise longue.

Diaper pattern. A design repeated to form a diagonal pattern.

"Distressed" furniture. Furniture that is purposely damaged and worn to make it look old.

Dough trough. A rectangular box with splayed sides and a cover, in which bread dough was mixed and raised.

Draw table. One with extension leaves which draw out from underneath the top.

Dry sink. A provincial piece of furniture. A cabinet with cupboards below and a deep gallery running around the top.

Dutch oven. (a) A shallow iron kettle with tightly fitted rimmed cover, which was placed in the coals for cooking; (b) A tin oven of reflector type for roasting before an open fire. *Not* a built-in brick bake oven found in the early kitchen fireplaces.

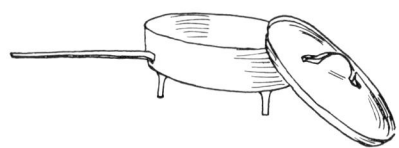

Early Georgian Period. 1714–1745, American.

East India print. An all-over pattern of Persian or Indian design printed on cotton. Used extensively for spreads and curtains in 18th century American houses.

Elizabethan Period. 1558–1603, English.

Empire Period, French. 1804–1815.

Empire Period, American. 1812–1890 (Victorian period).

Entry. The entrance area in an Early American type house.

Etagère. A 19th century rack or stack of shelves supported by columns or posts.

Eyebrow window. Low, long windows; also called lie-on-your-stomach windows, used on the second floor of a one and a half story house.

Fall-front. The hinged writing surface of a desk or secretary that folds up vertically when closed, and opens out flat for use.

Fanlight. Any window over a door. Formerly referred only to the fanshaped windows, but now inclusive of other shapes.

Feather-edge. A board trimmed to a fine edge fitting into a groove in another board.

Federal Period. From about the end of the Revolution to about 1830. Markedly classical style of furniture. The period of Duncan Phyfe.

Fiddle-back chair. A chair back whose center splat is fiddle-shaped. Usually found in Queen Anne or adaptations.

Field bed. A canopy bed of the smaller type; originally designed so that it could be moved about readily. Posts are lighter and whole bed less cumbersome than usual canopy bed.

Finial. A vertical decorative ornament, usually of wood or brass, used on the tops of highboys, secretaries, bedposts, etc.

FINIALS

Fireback. Castiron shield for protecting the bricks, and radiating heat, in the back part of a fireplace.

Flemish chair. Early chair of Dutch origin. Narrow, straight, carved back, heavy legs, usually scroll feet. Entire frame heavily carved.

Flemish scroll. A double scroll formed of two C-scrolls, one carved in the opposite direction to the other.

Fluting. Opposite of reeding. A series of concave, parallel grooves.

Food safe. A 19th century food storage cabinet on legs, usually with pierced tin paneled doors for ventilation and the exclusion of insects and rodents.

Form. The English name for a bench seat.

French Directoire Period. 1795–1799, including Consulate, 1799–1804.

French Provincial furniture. French country-made furniture from 17th century on.

Fretwork. Carved or sawed-out design in thin wood as an ornamentation. Used on shelf sides, galleries, chair backs, etc.

Fruitwood. Cherry, apple, and pear woods. They wear well and being hard woods polish well. Often used for Provincial pieces.

"Furniture checks." Linen, worsted, or silk fabric of colored checked design, popular in mid-18th century for window, bed, and curtain coverings.

Gable end. Either end of a house with a peaked roof.

Gallery. Standing rim on table top, or backing of sideboard top; of brass or wood— pierced or solid.

Gateleg table. Sometimes called a thousand-legged table. Has one or more hinged legs to support leaves.

Genre painting. Paintings from everyday life.

Georgian Period. 1714–1795. English Kings, George I, II, & III.

Gesso. Powdered plaster which is molded while soft into decorative relief forms. Colored or gilded after it is dry.

Girandole. A wall candle bracket often with mirror back. Later forms had circular convex mirror; sometimes called bull's eye mirror.

Girt. A horizontal beam framed into the posts of braced-frame house.

Goddard, John. A leading late 18th century cabinetmaker of Newport, R. I. who produced distinctive blockfront desks, cabinets, secretaries, and chests.

Gothic Period. English, 1485–1509. French, 12th, 13th, and 14th centuries.

Greek Revival Period. Followed American Georgian period; from about 1805–1830.

Hadley chest. Late 17th century type of chest with characteristic tulip carving in panels. Found originally in Hadley, Mass.

Hanging cupboard. A small accessory piece used for storing pipes, keys, and incidentals; found most often in hallways, kitchens, etc.

"Harlequin" furniture. A piece of furniture that serves a dual purpose, such as a combined table and library steps.

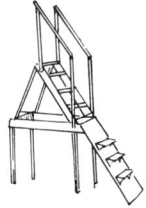

Hepplewhite, George. ?–1786. A famous English cabinetmaker who modified classic styles to produce furniture of great charm and elegance.

Highboy, or tallboy. A high chest of drawers, on legs, usually in two sections.

Hipped roof. A peaked roof whose gables have been sloped off.

Hogarth, William. English artist, 1697–1764.

Hooked rugs. Made by hand by pulling cloth through burlap or sacking with a large hooked needle. Of Scandinavian origin.

Hoop-back Windsors. Same as bow back. A Windsor in which the bentwood back runs in a continuous loop from one side of the seat to the other.

Hurricane globe. Glass chimney to prevent drafts from blowing out a candle.

Hutch table. From the French word *huche,* meaning trough. A table with a loose top mounted on a box whose ends are extended down to form feet.

Inlay. A means of decoration in wood by cutting a channel in the surface and filling it with wood, metal, etc. of a contrasting color or texture.

Irish Chippendale. Furniture made in the 18th century in Ireland by local craftsmen following Chippendale's designs.

Jacobean Period. 1603–1649. English.

Japanning. Varnish applied in several coats and dried by heat.

Joiner. A woodworker skilled in finer work than performed by a carpenter.

Joint stool. An early Jacobean stool with turned legs, tenoned joints, and stretchers.

Kas. A primitive Dutch cupboard or cabinet with painted or carved panels.

Keeping room. Term applied to the general living room of the Early American house where a family really lived (not the parlor).

Knotty pine. Pine with knots and other imperfections. Low-grade lumber.

Ladder-back chair. One with horizontal rails (like a ladder), in contrast to banister-back which has vertical ones.

Lazy Susan. A revolving tray mounted on a base so that it can be placed on a table.

Library steps. Portable steps used to reach upper part of bookcase.

Linenfold panel. Carved decoration wood or stone resembling folds of linen.

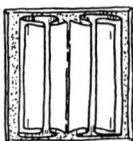

Linsey woolsey. Early American homespun material, coarse. Used commonly in every household for clothes, curtains, etc.

Lintel. A horizontal member spanning an opening, such as a fireplace.

Lion's paw foot. The foot of a chair leg shaped like a lion's paw.

Livery cupboard. An early English food cupboard.

Louis XIV Period. 1643–1715, French.

Louis XV Period. 1715–1774, French.

Louis XVI Period. 1774–1793, French.

Love seat. A sofa accommodating two persons.

Lowboy. Low chest or table with drawers derived from chest-on-legs, developed during Queen Anne period.

Mahogany. A reddish brown wood especially adapted to the making of furniture, having a fine texture and taking a polish well. Comes from the West Indies, Central and South America, and Africa.

Marquetry. Wood with an inlay of some other substance such as metal or stone.

McIntire, Samuel. 1757–1811. Architect, cabinetmaker, and carver of distinction. Born and lived all his life in Salem, Mass.

Meeting rail. The rails of a sash window which come together when the window is closed.

Mohair. A sturdy, woven fabric of cotton, linen, silk or wool combined with the hair of the Angora goat, having a pile. Used principally for upholstery.

Molding. Hollow or raised continuous strips of wood used as decoration, to hide joints, etc. May be applied or formed in base material.

Mushroom type chair. An armchair which has mushroom-shaped flat knobs at the tops of the arm posts.

Nutwood. Wood of any of the various nut trees.

One-post bed. One which has one side and one end fastened to the wall and therefore needs only one post to hold it up.

Ormolu. Ornamental gilded metal decoration used on French furniture.

Pad foot. A simple flattened end of a cabriole leg.

Palladian window. A group of three windows, the center one being higher and having a rounded top.

Pediment. On a house, the triangular mounting forming a decoration over a door or window; on furniture, the same form found on the tops of cabinets.

Pembroke table. A Chippendale innovation. Small rectangular table with drawer, and drop leaves supported by brackets.

Pennsylvania Dutch furniture. Made by 18th century German, Dutch, and Swiss settlers in eastern Pennsylvania, who used peasant designs on their furniture.

Philadelphia Chippendale. Work done by a group of cabinetmakers in Philadelphia in the style of Chippendale—middle 18th century.

Phyfe, Duncan. ?–1856. Scottish born, but began working in America in 1783. Leading maker of furniture based on Sheraton-Directoire styles, and later of Empire furniture style.

Pie-crust table. One with a round top and fluted edges, often scalloped in outline.

Pile weave. Fabric or carpet with upright ends. The pile is sometimes left uncut.

Pilgrim furniture. A loose term that has come to be applied to primitive furniture of the Pilgrim era.

Pillar-type legs. Chair or cabinet legs, square in section, and the same thickness throughout their length.

Plank floor. One made up of wide thick planks.

Platform rocker. A rocking chair mounted on a base to which it is attached by a spring or other device.

Pole screen. A small fire or light screen of wood or framed fabric mounted on a vertical pole or spindle, on which it can be adjusted for height.

Press bed. An early type of narrow bed that could be folded against the wall to make space in the room.

Press cupboard. A storage cupboard for linens, etc.

Pumpkin pine. From the *Strobus pinus* tree, the wood acquiring with time a mellow, yellow tone, warm and distinctive.

Queen Anne Period. 1702–1714, English.

Quillwork sconce. A decorative, framed wall hanging made as a reflector for candles held in side brackets. Usually a floral pattern made of paper (colored and curled), wax, wire, and mica.

Raffineé. (Fr.) Refined.

Rail. One of the two cross pieces of a frame or a panel.

Rake. On furniture, table or chair leg which is slanted or splayed and therefore not vertical. The legs of the American Windsor chair are raked.

Reeding. Opposite of fluting. A series of parallel, convex ribs.

Refectory table. Narrow, long dining table with heavy stretchers near the floor, such as used in monasteries.

Rep. A sturdy material of plain weave, reversible, with a heavy rib.

Ribband, or Ribbon-back. A ribbon-like form in chair back.

Riser. The vertical part of a stair step.

Rococo. An elaborate type of ornamentation consisting of rocks and shells, often with leaves and flowers intertwined.

Rushlight. A sort of candle made of swamp rush soaked in fat.

Rushlight holder. A claw-like device to contain the rushlight.

Sadiron. Early, old-fashioned iron for pressing clothes.

Salamander chair. An early type of arm chair with rush seat, beautiful turnings, and back slats forming silhouette of paired salamanders.

Satinwood. A light, honey-colored hard wood of fine lustrous grain coming from Ceylon, India, and the West Indies. Used extensively in 18th century English furniture.

Savery, William. A noted 18th century cabinetmaker of Philadelphia (1721–1787), famous for his elaborate Chippendale style highboys and lowboys.

Sawbuck. An early, crude table with a medial stretcher and legs formed in an X.

Scratch carving. Crude carving found on early pieces. Done with a V-chisel.

Secretary. A desk with a high top (usually pedimented) containing shelves behind doors, sometimes with drawers below.

Serpentine front. The double curve sometimes given to chest, desk, and sideboard fronts. Usually the center is convex and the ends concave.

Settee. A long seat with low back and arms, occasionally upholstered.

Settle. A movable long seat with a solid, high wooden back and ends to avert drafts.

Shaker furniture. Made by a religious group in the 19th century. Some of the most delightful but severely plain American provincial pieces were made by them.

Sheraton, Thomas. 1750–1806. Cabinetmaker, preacher, scholar. Made little furniture but published several books of designs from which the delicate classic Sheraton style was developed.

Slat-back chair. Same as ladder-back. Horizontal, flat or curved slat rails in chair back.

Spade foot. A rectangular tapered foot somewhat the shape of a spade.

Spandrel. Brass corner decorations on the face of a clock.

Spanish foot. Convex, ribbed, and spreading foot of chair leg, sometimes slightly scrolled or turned under.

Spatter work. Drops of paint spattered from a paint brush by hand.

Spindle. A long, thin, turned, round piece of wood, often tapered and shaped for use in chair backs, or as stretchers.

Splat. The wide vertical center piece of wood in a chair back.

Splay. Rake. Splayed leg is one extending outward from its attachment.

Spool bed. A bed whose head and foot boards are composed of or decorated with spool-shaped turnings.

Spoon back. A Queen Anne characteristic of chair backs shaped to human contours.

Squab. Stuffed, loose cushion used on chair seat. Originally used in 17th and 18th centuries.

Stair rods. Rods used to hold a stair carpet in position.

Stencil. A design applied by daubing paint over a cut-out in heavy paper.

Stile. One of the two upright pieces of a frame or a panel.

Stretcher. A wooden support extending between legs of tables or chairs.

Stuart. 1603–1649. English Stuart Kings—James I, Charles I, Charles II, James II, Early Jacobean, Cromwellian, Restoration).

Swan-neck pediment. One which is made up of two S-curves, facing each other. Found over Georgian doorways, and on tops of Queen Anne or Chippendale cabinets and secretaries.

Tambour. A flexible sliding door or cover made of narrow strips of wood glued to a backing of linen or duck.

Tavern table. An early, rectangular table, used in taverns. Made with a drawer in the apron; with or without stretchers.

Tester Bed. The word tester comes from an old French word *"testiere"* meaning a head piece or helmet, and came to mean, in England, the frame for holding the canopy over a highpost bed.

Thimble foot. Same as spade foot, but more often turned than square.

Tilt-top table. One with top hinged to the pedestal so that it may be tilted.

Toile de Jouy. Realistic designs of scenes, flowers, or landscapes printed on fine cotton. Process originated at Jouy, France, near Paris about 1760. Good reproductions are made today in wallpaper as well as in fabric.

Tôle. (Fr.) Painted tinware.

Tory chimney. A house chimney that is painted white with a band of black around the top.

Trammel. An adjustable iron hook for hanging pots over a fire.

Tread. The horizontal part of a stair step.

Trestle table. One with the top mounted on two flat, wide legs, joined by a stretcher.

Tripod table. One with the top mounted on a center pedestal, having three legs.

Trumpet leg. A decorative turning shaped like a trumpet with the mouth upward.

Trundle bed. A low small bed which could be rolled under a high bed for storage during the day.

Tudor. 1485–1603. English, comprising reigns of Henry VII, Henry VIII, Edward VI, Mary and Elizabeth.

Turkey work. Worsted embroidery done on canvas, popular in 17th century.

Turn-up French foot. A scroll or spiral foot, or a swept-out foot as used by Hepplewhite.

Tuxedo sofa. An upholstered sofa with flat, outward curved ends.

Underbrace. A stretcher for strengthening the legs of a piece of furniture.

Valance. Ruffle or skirt used on lower part of Colonial bed; or decorative piece hung from the top of the window over draperies.

Vase back. Outline of center splat resembles a vase in shape. A characteristic of the Queen Anne chair.

Veneer. Very thin decorative wood glued onto a solid wood backing.

Victorian period. The era of Queen Victoria's reign, 1837–1901, marked by fussy, tasteless, and extravagant furniture.

Wagon chair. A double chair with short legs, rush or splint seat, usually with ladder back, used for additional seats in a wagon.

Wag-on-wall. Very early wall clock with exposed weights, hung high up on the wall.

Wainscot. Wall paneling.

Wainscot chair. An arm chair with a paneled back and solid wooden seat. The earliest type of armchair in America.

Welsh dresser. Type of cupboard, with open shelves above, and cupboards or drawers, or both, below.

Western Reserve. That section of Ohio state originally a part of Connecticut and settled by immigrants from New York and New England.

Whatnot. A curio display set of shelves usually graduated in size.

William-and-Mary Period. 1688–1702, English.

Windsor chair. Originating in England. American type developed in Philadelphia after 1725. Bentwood frame with spindle back, saddle-shaped seat, splayed legs. Made in rocker, arm chair, settee, etc., styles, sometimes with bamboo turnings.

BIBLIOGRAPHY

The Encyclopedia of Furniture—Aronson, Joseph, Crown Publishers, New York, 1938.

Colonial Furniture in America—Lockwood, Luke Vincent, Charles Scribner's Sons, New York, 1901.

Furniture of the Pilgrim Century—Nutting, Wallace, Marshall Jones Co., Boston, 1921.

The Period Furniture Handbook—Gould, Mr. and Mrs. C. Glen, Dodd, Mead & Co., New York, 1928.

Early American Furniture—Cornelius, Charles O., The Century Co., New York, 1926.

Furniture of the Olden Time—Morse, Frances C., The Macmillan Co., New York, 1937.

The House of Simplicity—Seal, Ethel Davis, The Century Co., New York, 1926.

Furnishing the Little House—Seal, Ethel Davis, The Century Co., New York, 1924.

Genuine Antique Furniture—De Bles, Arthur, Thomas Y. Crowell Co., New York, 1929.

Shaker Furniture—Andrews, Edward D., and Faith, Yale University Press, New Haven, 1937.

The Colonial and Federal House—Newcomb, Rexford, J. B. Lippincott Co., Philadelphia, 1933.

Your Own Home—Robinson, Ethel Fay, and Thomas, Viking Press, New York, 1941.

The Personality of a House—Post, Emily, Funk and Wagnalls Co., New York, 1948.

The Complete Book of Interior Decorating—Derieux, Mary, and Stevenson, Isabelle, Greystone Press, 1948.

Essentials and Principles of Interior Decoration—Miller, Gladys, Doubleday and Co., New York, 1946.

Furniture for Your Home—Miller, Gladys, M. Barrows & Co., New York, 1946.

New Geography of American Antiques—Drepperd, Carl, and Guild, Lurelle Van Arsdale, Doubleday & Co., New York, 1948.

Living With Antiques—ed. by Winchester, Alice, Robert M. McBride Co., New York, 1948.

Furnishing the Colonial and Federal House—McClelland, Nancy, J. B. Lippincott Co., Philadelphia, 1947.

The Collecting of Antiques—Singleton, Esther, The Macmillan Co., New York, 1937.

The Pageant of America, Volume XII—Yale University Press, New Haven, 1927.

Early American Craftsmen—Dyer, Walter A., The Century Co., New York, 1915.

Early American Pottery and China—Spargo, John, The Century Co., New York, 1926.

The Practical Book of Learning Decoration and Furniture—Holloway, Edward Stratton, J. B. Lippincott Co., Philadelphia, 1926.

The Practical Book of Early American Arts and Crafts—Eberlein, Harold Donaldson, and McClure, Abbott, J. B. Lippincott Co., Philadelphia, 1916.

The Practical Book of American Antiques—Garden City Publishing Co., Garden City, N. Y., 1926.

Old American Houses and How To Restore Them—Williams, Henry Lionel and Ottalie K., Doubleday & Co., New York, 1946.

INDEX

ACKNOWLEDGMENTS

The authors extend their sincere thanks to the following individuals and firms for their kind interest and cooperation in the preparation of this book.

For permission to use interior photographs of their homes we are indebted to Mrs. Aline Bernstein and Mrs. Ethel Frankau, Armonk, N. Y. (page 153); Mr. Joseph Downs, North Guilford, Conn. (pages 7, 66); Mr. B. F. Hunter, Lebanon, Ind. (pages 142-146); and Mr. Howard C. Sherwood, Setauket, N. Y. (pages 71, 157, 159; also jacket and frontispiece photographs).

To Miss Alice Winchester, Editor, ANTIQUES Magazine, New York, we owe our thanks for supplying the Sherwood prints. The photographs on pages 39, 42, 138 and 178 are from the collection of The Metropolitan Museum of Art and were secured through the cooperation of Mr. Joseph Downs, Curator, The American Wing.

The following firms graciously allowed the use of material from their files:

FABRICS
F. Schumacher & Co., New York, N. Y. (pages 85-88).

FLOOR COVERINGS
Armstrong Cork Co., Lancaster, Pa. (page 26).
A. & M. Karagheusian, Inc. (Gulistan), New York, N. Y. (page 101).
David Kennedy, Inc., Brooklyn, N. Y. (pages 9, 166).
Mohawk Carpet Mills, Inc., Amsterdam, N. Y. (pages 106-109).
F. Schumacher & Co., New York, N. Y. (pages 103, 104).
The Tile-Tex Co., Inc., Chicago Heights, Ill. (page 15).

FURNITURE
Baker Furniture Co., Grand Rapids, Mich. (page 44).
Biggs Antique Co., Richmond, Va. (pages 62, 125, 215).
Bodart Furniture Co., New York, N. Y. (page 207).
Brandt Cabinet Works, Inc., Hagerstown, Md. (pages 54-56, 80, 198).
Charak Furniture Co., Inc., New York, N. Y. (pages 134, 139, 177, 184, 206, 210).
Conant Ball Co., Gardner, Mass. (pages 32, 173, 183).
Drexel Furniture, Inc., Drexel, N. C. (pages 204, 213).
Heywood-Wakefield Co., Gardner, Mass. (pages 23, 123, 168-171, 216).
Kittinger Co., Inc. (Colonial Williamsburg Reproductions), Buffalo, N. Y. (pages 45, 46, 61).
The Mengel Co., Louisville, Ky. (pages 77, 179, 187).
The Mersman Bros. Corp., Celina, Ohio (pages 53, 59, 130, 202, 203).

ACKNOWLEDGMENTS

Morgan Furniture Co., Asheville, N. C. (pages 25, 185).
The Statton Furniture Mfg. Co., Hagerstown, Md. (page 36).
Union-National, Inc., Jamestown, N. Y. (page 209).

WALL COVERINGS

W. H. S. Lloyd Co., Inc., New York, N. Y. (pages 93 top, 94).
F. Schumacher & Co., New York, N. Y. (pages 93 bottom, 97-99).
Standard Coated Products (Sanitas), New York, N. Y. (pages 5, 100, 191).
Richard E. Thibaut, Inc., New York, N. Y. (page 96).
The Wallpaper Institute, New York, N. Y. (pages 95, 102).

MISCELLANEOUS

Friedman Bros. Decorative Arts, Inc. (Col. Williamsburg Reproduction Mirrors), New York, N. Y. (pages 136, 137).
Gulf Oil Corp. (Hunter Clock Collection), Pittsburgh, Pa. (pages 142-146).
The Magnavox Co., Fort Wayne, Ind. (pages 128, 129).
North American Electric Lamp Co. (Nalco), St. Louis, Mo. (pages 114, 117).
Edward P. Paul & Co., Inc. (Lamps), New York, N. Y. (page 118).
Stromberg-Carlson Co., Rochester, N. Y. (page 127).

PHOTOGRAPHERS

H. Bagby, Richmond, Va. (page 125); Paul Davis, Boston, Mass. (pages 23, 123, 168, 171, 216); Andrea DeCook, New York, N. Y. (pages 9, 166); Robert F. Ganley, New York, N. Y. (pages 7, 66); Hedrich-Blessing, Ltd., Chicago, Ill. (pages 25, 185); Charles Kanarian, New York, N. Y. (page 96); Dale Rooks, Grand Rapids, Mich. (page 183); Richard Averill Smith, New York, N. Y. (page 5); Todd Studios, St. Louis, Mo. (page 114); Wurts Bros., New York, N. Y. (page 71).

Thanks are due also to the following firms, whose excellent material it was not possible to fit into the book: Bigelow-Sanford Carpet Co., Inc.; The Birge Company; Burlington Mills Corp.; Cabin Crafts, Inc.; Carpet Institute, Inc.; Carson, Pirie, Scott & Co.; Cyrus Clark Co., Inc.; Colonial Manufacturing Co.; Columbia Mills, Inc.; H. T. Cushman Manufacturing Co.; The Essex Institute; Goodall Fabrics; Grand Rapids Chair Co.; Katzenbach & Warren, Inc.; Kent-Coffey Manufacturing Co.; The Klearflax Linen Looms, Inc.; The Kling Factories; Lexington Chair Co.; Louisville Textiles, Inc.; C. H. Masland & Sons, Inc.; Ogden Manufacturing Co.; Packard-Malloy, Inc.; The Paraffine Companies, Inc.; Ed Roos Co.; L. & J. G. Stickley, Inc.; Thomas Strahan Co.; Seth Thomas Clocks; Tomlinson; The United States Stoneware Co.; White Furniture Co.; W. F. Whitney Co., Inc.; York Wallpaper Co.